DEEP CALLS
UNTO DEEP

DEEP CALLS UNTO DEEP

How Deep Do You Want To Go With God?

DONNA BLOOD

XULON PRESS

Xulon Press
2301 Lucien Way #415
Maitland, FL 32751
407.339.4217
www.xulonpress.com

Unless otherwise indicated, Scripture quotations taken from the King James Version (KJV) – *public domain.*

The Dictionaries used; the Reader's Digest Great Encyclopedic Dictionary, and the Vine's Expository Dictionary of the New Testament by Hendrickson.

Paperback ISBN-13: 978-1-6628-3381-6
Ebook ISBN-13: 978-1-6628-3382-3

I dedicate my book to my father, as his life demonstrated he knew God; so that is what I desired to do even at a young age and to find God for myself.

I also wish to thank my daughter, Charlene for her advice and knowledge of the computer, working with the Publisher; as well as our Granddaughter who added her talent in designing the covers and illustrations.

Table of Contents

Foreword

The Statue of Liberty

Freedom; Just as the Statue of Liberty represents freedom in America and a good life, so did my father find a good life here in America, coming from the Smoland area of Sweden, where potatoes and lingonberries were the staples of life. But what he brought with him was freedom from the bondage of sin and was set free through a decision he made to receive Jesus Christ into his heart at a camp meeting that had come to town. My father's very life showed me that he knew God; so that's what I desired too, and decided to find God for myself even at a young age.

The way to God is through His Son; just like it says in the Word of God that, "No man can come to the Father but by me, Jesus." John 6:44

Freedom is a choice, as God will not force anyone; He will accept any person if they choose to come to Him through Jesus, His Son. It's all by Grace and not by what good we do.

The sacrifice of God's Son on the cross was in our place, for us and Jesus was willing. His Holy Blood met the requirement of the Law to save us from Hell's destruction and washed us clean; just as if we've never sinned. Free from a guilty conscience. What Joy!
Hebrews 9:22

God's heart desire is for a person to come back to the one who He has created. For a personal loving relationship that He offers, and one in whom you can trust; and it's everlasting.

One day God said to me; "Where does it say in the Word that I will never leave you nor forsake you"? I immediately said, "I don't know." But I found it in Hebrews 13:5. God promises that He will never abandon you so you can trust Him, just like He said in His Word."

How much does God love you? This much; "For God so loved the world that He gave His only begotten Son, that whosoever believes in Him should not perish, but have everlasting life." John 3:16

Preface

T wo things happened in my life that led me to write a book, because it never was in my thinking to write one.

For 30 years I was a volunteer along with ten others with the International Women's AGLOW Prison Ministry; from 1982 to 2011, when I resigned. This was an experience that I needed for what was to come.

On May 5, 2015, that's five years later, I was leaving the room from a time I spent with the Lord and I heard Him say, "If you come back tomorrow at this same time, I will give you a Course on Love," "I can do that, I said." So I showed up at the appointed time and sat down and it didn't take long to see that He was God, talking about His love and His Son. "OH, I thought, I better write this down." So we finished that day.

The next day was the same, He just started talking and I would write it down. The next day came and again it went the same way, and the next and the next and the next; until it came to the 20th day. It just amazes me how long it was just on one subject, and you will see for yourself.

The next thing that came to mind was that this teaching didn't come just for me. It was to give away! So I decided to break it up to teach it to the church we were attending; and I was happy that I had done that.

Now that I'm 83 years of age, I was thinking to myself, "Now my work is done." "Immediately I heard inside of me, "Not so; use the tools that you have." WOW, I knew right away what He wanted was to write it in a book for more people to read. And that's how this book came into being.

You see, I had written material over those years during the time I was a volunteer in the Prison, to help fill the book; besides the teaching called "The Course on Love."

What you won't want to miss is "The Miracle of the Yellow Rose" at the end of the book.

Chapter 1

The Course On Love

Day 1

"And GOD said: "Love never fails."

"It begins and ends in faithfulness. God's love is that kind of love. The world's kind of love cannot come close to the measure that I am capable of; the fullness that you can obtain through my Son, Jesus.

No doubt the skeptics won't even consider doing this, but my people that have experienced my fullness knows this to be true.

But to those who seek, they shall find and those who open up their hearts to know Me, will have an experience, even to the measure of being filled with His love and My presence."

Hebrews 13:5; Matthew 7:7; Deuteronomy 7:9;
Jeremiah 29:11-14; Hebrews 10:23; Ephesians 1:23

Day 2

"Fullness is the key to receive His glory."

"This isn't a man made concoction, tradition or dream made up. It is in its broadest sense when one experiences the presence of the Lord.

To be sure no one can catch this on the run. It is developed over a period of time, spending time in the presence of God.

The very oil of the presence of the Holy Spirit poured out lavishly, definitely and not sparingly. So who would like to have this Glory poured out upon yourself; and isn't it the Holy Spirit's job to do just that?

Why not linger and wait on God. Time spent with Him is always profitable. The way to Glory is through Him that is All Glorious! "

Psalm 8:4,5; Psalm 16:11b; John 1:14; John 1:33; Acts 1:5; Ephesians 3:19; 2Corinthians 4:6

Day 3

"Love never fades or diminishes because it is eternal life, flowing from the Son to whom He wills by My Spirit."

"I Am that fountain of life. A gift to be received; and whoever will, can come and drink from the water of life freely.

The world knows nothing of this life because it isn't earthly, but heavenly. To all those who believe can come and be refreshed whenever he chooses. Yes, I give you choices.

Behold, I stand before you this day saying, I hold in my hand curses and blessings.

Choose life. My life is never demanding. It is always on the basis of your free will."

John 1:12; John 4:14; John 11:25; John 18:36; Matthew 10:8; Jeremiah 31:3; Hebrews 13:5; John 1:4; Revelation 3:20; Deuteronomy 30:19

Day 4

"Faith works by love"

"Do you remember that I told you that? Doubt will kill faith faster than anything else. However, when truth is revealed, it dispels the darkness of doubt. It eliminates the barrier and destroys its bondage.

The love of the Lord reveals truth to those who spend time with Him and listens; because of the hardness of heart, one cannot receive this truth;

Truth sets us free, no longer hindered by the lying spirit. Free to receive revelation and knowledge, the hidden things of God; and as I said before, the hard hearted is unable to receive; but the love of God does His good work in the heart. Softens so one can hear and this is the work of the Holy Spirit."

Galatians 5:6; John 8:32; Ezekiel 3:26;
Romans 10:17

Day 5

"My Love for you never grows cold, Indifferent, complacent nor dull of hearing. In hearing, you respond to the love that I have poured out on the Cross. Love comes from hearing."

"All that I have I have given you, that you may abound in His love as well. You see that I am not selfish. Always my heart is towards those that I have created. Yes, for Glory. To be My own and to live in My Kingdom forever.

Satan has his agenda but so do I.

Never fear who is the strongest or the Greatest. If you do succumb to his whims you are done for; not being able to rise unless I intervene.

Trust and obedience to My Truth of the Word will always rise triumphantly; but My people lack knowledge" "Like it says, "My people are destroyed for lack of knowledge." Soon the days will come to an end and will I find faith on earth? "

"There will be distress of nations that the world has never known. Only the faithful few will survive. Be not discouraged; for I have overcome the world. To this end have I come; you bet this is Love in Action."

Hebrews 13:8; Colossians 1:13; John 10:10, 1John 4:4; Hosea 4,6; Luke 21:25; John 16:33; Malachi 3:6; Romans 10:17; Revelation 4:11 Hosea 4:6; Matthew 24:4-7; Proverbs 4: John 16:33

Day 6

"The Kind of Love that I desire you to have is the unlimited grace, mercy and truth. For which you cannot accomplish anything without."

"All the more of love, the more of grace will be the power to overcome as I am within you. To know Me more than you know yourself. Forever changed into My Glory! Glory that exceeds human reasoning and understanding.

Be near Me child for this is for you, My beloved children of the Father. For those whom He has given Me, I will not lose and I will raise them up on the last day.

The love that dwells within you is everlasting; So faithful am I. Continue to be faithful and I will reward you.

Nothing passes Me by that I do not know. Believe me and be faithful unto the end and I will give you the crown of life."

"So shall my word be that goes forth out of my mouth. My love; for you will go from glory to glory."

1John 4:4; John 1:17; Romans 5:17-21, John 15:5,7; 1Corinthians 6:14; James 1:12; Isaiah 55:11; John 6:39; 2nd Corinthians 5:17; Romans 3:24 James 1:12; Rev 2:10; Isaiah 55:11; Psalm 23:6

Day 7

"Love is the key"

"Love is never difficult or hard to give away because it is My character.

It's genuinely sincere and compassionate; truly concerned about the well being of people. Yes, everything you are concerned about, the God of love is too.

So when the love of God is shed abroad in your heart it is the same that God has.

Time spent in MY Word feeds your spirit. It builds your faith up and the Spirit works in your spirit to give the love of God away. Don't try to figure this out because it happens automatically.

Love never changes; It is kind and does not insist on its own way. Love is the Key to freedom and a stable Life. For in Me do you live and move and have your being.

Come to Me. Spend time with Me and fill up with the fullest measure of My love."

Romans 5:5,8; Romans 8:18; Romans 9:23;
Psalm 27:1; Romans 13:10; Psalm 145:20;
John 14:26; John 15:13; Romans 10:17; John 1:16; John 1:14; Malichi 3:6; Ephesians 1:23; Ephesians 4:13; Hebrews 13:8

Day 8

"God has promised,"

"That through faith in the Name of Jesus, we are given the same inheritance given to Abraham, the seed of promise.

A principle of Spiritual life as imparted to the believer, which abides in Christ. Surely this is love personified to include All the Nations of the World through Abraham's seed. Blessings untold, lavishly poured out to those of faith.

My purpose for dying was to bring the fullness of my love for a life of abundance. As I said, to go from glory to glory in the fullness of My Spirit, are untold riches of my Grace, have I given to all who can receive.

Come to Me and receive. You will be blessed."

Hebrews 11:8; Galatians 3:7; Galatians 3:16; Galatians 3:28,29; John 1:16; John 1:14

Day 9

"My love is different from human love."

"It is transparent and sees the deep need in which no man can comprehend.

Deep calls unto deep. How deep Do You Want To Go With God? My riches are unlimited, Yes, even in power.

How much do you expect from God?

See I am sending the Holy Spirit and through Him My life and love will fill you for the abundant life. Take and drink. Take and drink if you are thirsty; for freely I give, freely shall you receive.

Remember, do this in remembrance of Me, who has given you everything you will ever need. Come My beloved and be mine, forever."

Psalm 42:7,8; Ephesians 1:17-19; Philippians 4:19; Romans 8:11,26; Ephesians :3:15-21; Luke 22:18-20

Day 10

"The feeling that comes upon you when you are in the presence of the one you love is from above. You are ordained to love.

The Father's love needs that response from the one whom He has created. There is a place within you especially made for Him to fill, to live in, move in; doing His good will and His pleasure.

One can resist and not allow Him access into your heart. You have a free will. Furthermore, it is My divine nature that will come and bring a new change in you. A New Spirit will I give you, so we can be one.

Behold, I stand at the door and knock. If anyone hears My voice and opens the door, I will come in and sup with him and he with Me." I will not disappoint you."

Psalm 16:11; Acts 17:28; 2Corinthians 5:17; Ezekiel 36:24,25; Revelation 3:20; Romans 10:13

Day 11

"Choose life."

"The love of the world is vain because the love of God's not in him.

Love of the brethren is of God. He who receives me, receives the love of the Father. We go hand in hand for we are one.

Oneness with Me fulfills the law; It is called the Law of Life.

"For I am the way, the truth and the life; no one comes to the Father except by Me." Choose this day whom you will serve; Choose Jesus the one and only true God.

Forever I have loved you, and that's before the world began. you are ordained of God to love Him with all your heart, soul, strength and mind and your neighbor as yourself."

John 10:25-27; John 17:21; Romans 8:2; John 14:6; Ephesians 1:4; Luke 10:27

Day 12

"No man lays down his life for a friend unless he so loves him; that he is willing to do so."

"The comfort that you seek is in the saving love of the Lord Jesus. So come to Me and receive all that the Father has for you in the Name of Jesus.

His love flows freely Like a river and ends not. Like a mighty river, ever flowing ceaselessly. Grace is My way for you to receive. So come and experience all that My love has to offer."

John 15:13; Psalm 23; John 7:38; Psalm 1:2,3; John 14:6; Mark 10:15

God's Love Flows like a River

Day 13

And God said, "I have two exercises."

"The following is an exercise you can use to stretch yourself in the practice of obedience to love.

First—Be attentive; means pay attention to what the Word of God tells you to Do.

Second – On My honor, I will honor those who are attentive; Means pay attention to Me.

Come and empty yourself out and drink in the presence of the Holy Spirit. He will fill you up. You must be empty of self in order to be filled. You must invite Him.

Love is a free gift, given and shed abroad in your heart by My Spirit, then you will be able to hear My voice better and you will have the love of God to give away; because you cannot give out what you don't have. So recall the first thing:

Is to examine the Word to find out your responsibility, which is the first commandment. "You shall love the Lord your God with all of your Heart and with all of your strength". This is the first commandment."

"That's paying attention to the second part of obedience. The second commandment is easy and that's loving others; Giving out of what you have received."

James 1:22; James 4:8; Romans 5:5; Revelation 3:29: John 1:33; Mark 12:30,31

Day 14

"Love never fails, so you can count on Me who is love , to be faithful."

"Love draws out the best in people. That's why I came, to bring the best out of you. "He that has the Son has life, and he who has not the Son, has not life."

The life of love is the power in which to live by. The commandment commands the love to be lived out in one's life. Life and love are the greatest of all gifts.

I am come that you might have life, and the love of God will be manifested in you.

Come to Me and draw on this free gift of life and love."

1Corinthians 13:8; 1John 5:12; 1Corinthians 15:57; Zechariah 10:12; 1st Corinthians 13:3; John 10:10

Day 15

"Love fulfills the Law"

"No other love is greater than the one who dies for them.

I am He that willingly laid down My life out of love for the brethren, whom We have created In His image did We make them." Love fulfills the Law, it is enough.

Take for example your love for your children must be the same as others, like they were your own.

The Father knows His own and has given them unto Me."

My response;
Take my life and let it be, consecrated Oh Lord unto thee.

"Let it be as you have said."

John 15:13; John 12:31; Genesis 1:27; Galatians 6:2; Matthew 7:11; John 17:24

Day 16

"I know the thoughts that I have towards you; thoughts of peace and not of evil and to give you an expected end."

"The coming of the Son of man was twofold. To forgive sins yes, but to impart a life that is full of glory, love and peace.

You know why Satan came, don't you?

"But to kill, steal and destroy. I am come that you might have life and have it more abundantly."

Days are full of choices; time and grace to fulfill your every wish.

I have chosen you that you might live in harmony with My Spirit, for I have sent Him to be of help to you.

So choose this day whom you will serve; self or Me. I will never disappoint you."

Jeremiah 29:11; John 17:22; John 1"0:10; 3rdJohn 2; John 16:7,13; Joshua 24:15

Day 17

"Come unto Me all you who labor and are heavy laden, and I will give rest and comfort to your souls. Take my yoke upon you and learn of Me, for I am meek and lowly of heart."

"See how He loves His own. They live in Him and His Kingdom forever.

For so long I have held out My hand to a wandering sheep to come and be a part of My flock. My flock hears My voice and they come and go in safety. Green pastures of prosperity and good health is mine to give; but no one heeds My call.

The Shepherd of the sheep is a good shepherd. Not like a hireling because they do not care nor is concerned for the well being of the flock. The good Shepherd knows his sheep by name and claims them to be his own. Forsake not the good Shepherd and He will not forsake you."

Proverbs 1:24; John 11:14; Hebrews 13:5; Matthew 11:28-30; Acts 17:28; Colossians 1:13

Day 18

My Response:

I was thinking about Righteousness. What is it that makes me right with God? I am loved and that's why I am forgiven. Forgiven, cleansed and made whole like Jesus.

Just like a New Creature as everything becomes new. Nothing is the same as before, because of the Lordship of Jesus' life and nature in us, from sin to righteousness; being right with God by faith.

What a wonderful gift to receive, because it's nothing we have done to deserve this gift, but by the mercy and grace of God made it so.

Jesus responds, "Beloved and accepted just as if you've never done anything wrong. A clear conscience and a pure heart before Me in love; a loving relationship to experience and to give away.

So it is with My Father's love. We have agreed upon this; to send Me to die in your place. My blood of sacrifice, acceptable to God, to pay the debt you owe. For the wages of sin is death; but the gift of God is eternal life, now and forever."

2Corinthians 5:21; 2Corinthians 5:17;Romans 3:21-27; John 10:17,18; Ephesians 1:6,7; Romans 6:22,23

Day 19

"I AM what I say I AM."

"The one whom I have chosen will be as I AM. Holy, spotless and without blemish, My bride.

It is my church that I have chosen. Undefiled and full of Grace, without condemnation; and when you see Me, you will be as I am. Clothed in My image of GLory for a life that is sustained forever.

I AM what I say I AM; Oh, to believe in the One True God, who is "The Great I AM."

To whom he will belong to, depends on the Decision they make . Will it be you?"

Romans 12:1; Revelation 21:1; Colossians 1:18; Matthew 16:18; 1John 3:2; Revelation 1:8; Revelation 1:18

Day 20

"I have come to you these days as light upon your darkness. It is for your benefit that I have done so."

"Causes of darkness will bring you back into it, but a determined spirit will maintain the light to remain. Where does one Receive this Light? Through My Son, Jesus.

He is the light that shines upon your pathway; an overcomer in all respects. He will teach you and guide you with the eye of My Spirit, says the Lord. Together with His loving kindness and tender mercy shall you be safe and prosperous.

Be attentive to the Words of Life and to My presence.

For In Me do you live and move and have your being. Without Me you can do nothing."

"So it will be as I said."

The End of 20 days
John 8:12; John 12:35; John 14:16; Psalm 16:11; John 6:63; Acts 7:28

Chapter 2

"A Word From the Lord"

"In as much as you have chosen to draw near to Me, I will draw near to you. Here is My heart's desire; that you and I become one. Nowhere in the scripture does it say go it alone. No, not at all does it say this.

This is for your benefit and not mine.

This love that I have for you is never ending. It will never diminish nor fade away; as it says in the scripture, "I Will Never Leave You Nor Forsake You." I am faithful and as you yield to Me in your heart or spirit, I can be to you everything you need.

Call upon me and I will answer you; because you have set your love upon Me; therefore I will deliver you. I will set you up on high because you have known My name; But oneness I mean is forever."

James 4:8: John 15:5; Hebrews 13:5; Psalm 91:15 Romans 6:13; Psalm 90:2; 1st John 5:11-13

My Response:
If God is from everlasting to everlasting; and you are in Him, and He is in you, then the Oneness is meant forever."

My husband and I have been members of several churches over our 65 years of marriage; and One Pastor related to His congregation, His firm belief was that a person doesn't need to do anything to be saved.

That statement I'm sorry to say, has stuck with me; only because I believe there is. John 1:11 and 12 comes to mind which talks about John the Baptist, being a witness to the coming Jesus. "He came unto His own Israel, and His own received Him not." But as many as received Him, gave He the power to become sons of God. John 1:12

So as I was rereading the "Course on Love," I was thinking about the word "Receive."

Then I recalled what a leader at one of many conferences I had attended too, had made a comment just before the meeting was about to begin, He said,

"If you don't get anything out of this meeting just remember this one thing, You Have What You Received." John 1:16

Then my thoughts went back to the "Course on Love," and I was thinking, just how many times did God say the word, receive?

It was 12 times. Here they are as follows; God Said:

Day 1 –"To Receive His fullness is the key to His Glory."
Ephesians 1:23; Ephesians 4:13

Day 3 -"Eternal Life Is A Gift To Receive."
1John 5:11-13

Day 4 "Free To Receive Revelation and Knowledge."
Ephesians 1:17

Day 8–"To go from Glory to Glory in the fullness of His Spirit, are untold riches of His Grace, has He given To All Who Can Receive." 2Corinthians 3:18

Day 9 "Through the Holy Spirit He freely gives." 1John 2:20

Day 10 -"There's a place in you for God to fill, dwell, live in, move in, work in doing His will and pleasure; If you have Him in Your heart."
Acts 17:28

"My life and love is to those who are thirsty; for freely He gives and freely you shall receive." Matthew 10:8

Day 11–"He Who Received Me, Jesus, receives The Love of the Father; For We are One. Oneness with Me Fulfills The Law."

John 10:30; 1John 5:12: 2Corinthians 5:17:
Romans 13:10;

(A Spiritual Law causes us to miss the grave and goes up to heaven and not down to Hell; just like the Law of Gravity)

Day 12 -"Jesus offers saving Love; so come to Me and receive All that the Father has for you, in the Name of Jesus." Matthew 7:7

"Grace is God's way for you to receive. So come and experience All that My love has to offer." 2Corinthians 6:1,2

Day 13 – "Receiving Jesus, then you have the Holy Spirit and will fill you with Love to do the 2nd Commandment; to love your neighbor giving out what you received.
1Corinthians 12:13

Day 14 – "If You haven't Received the Son, Jesus, then His Life Isn't In you. Come draw on this free gift of Life and Love." 1John 5:11:13; John 7:37

Day 17 – "Take; Receive My yoke Upon you and Learn of Me." Matthew 11:29

Day 20 – "Where does one Receive Light? In My Son, Jesus." John 1:4,7, 12

My thoughts:
On Day 11, "The Lord said a new thing I never heard before; that "In receiving Jesus into their heart, fulfills the Law of Oneness." (I mention other Spiritual Laws later)

There is no doubt in my mind that everything that was spoken to me is confirmed by God's Word; and the most important thing to me was the word, "Receive," it was said twelve times.

I don't know about you, but I'm going to agree with God's Word over any Pastor that tells me that there's nothing one needs to do to have Salvation.

Romans 10:9,10; John 1:12; John 3:3-8; Revelation 3:20

And by the way – There's more than one thing Jesus came to save us from besides just our sins. Yes, but He also came to give us a New Life; and how do we get this new life? Through God's Son, Jesus.

Jesus said to Nicodemus, "You must be born again."
"How can this be, he said?"
Jesus answered, "the Spirit is Spirit and the flesh is flesh."

The change must be in our spirit, or heart. Spirit and heart means the same thing.
John 3:3-8

"For the Holy Spirit of Life In Christ Jesus, we become a New Creature. Old things pass away and behold, All things become new. "For the Law of The Spirit of Life In Christ Jesus, Has made me Free From The Law of Sin and Death."

2nd Corithians 5:17; Romans 8:2

Chapter 3

The Law of Oneness

"He Who Has Life Has the Son,
and he Who has not The Son, has not Life."
1st John 5:11

A s God himself expressed to me; "Salvation is based on your Decision to Receive Jesus into your heart as Lord and Savior." In receiving, your spirit gets changed for the Holy Spirit of Life in Christ Jesus, becoming One." John 1:12

If you haven't made this decision of choosing the life of Jesus, you can come to Him now; for He said," I will in no wise, or way, cast you out." Matthew 11:28

So Listen to what He is saying to you;

"Behold I stand at the door and knock, if any man hears my voice and opens the door, I will come into him and sup with him and he with Me." Revelation 3:20

"For God so loved the world, that He gave his only begotten son, that Whosoever, that's you, believes in Him, shall not perish, but have everlasting life." Choose Life! John 3:16

"If you confess with your mouth the Lord Jesus, and shall believe in your heart that God has raised Him, Jsesus, from the dead, you shall be saved." Romans 10:10

The following scriptures confirm the "Law of Oneness. "

"That in the dispensation of the fullness of times He might gather in one all things in Christ, both which are in heaven and which are on earth; even In Him." Ephesians 1:9

"In whom, Jesus, also we have obtained an inheritance, being predestined according to the purpose of Him who works all things after the counsel of His own will." Ephesians 1:10,11

"I am crucified with Christ, nevertheless I live; yet not I but Christ lives in Me; and the life which I now live in the flesh I live by the faith of the Son of God, who loved me, and gave himself for Me." Galatians 2:20

"Know ye not, that so many of us were baptized into Jesus Christ, were baptized into His death." Romans 6:3

"For in Him we live, and move and have our being." Acts 17:28

Oneness Con't.

"But as many as received Him, to them He gave the power to become the sons of God, even to those that believe in His Name." John 1:12

"And this is the record that God has given to us eternal life, and this life is in His Son. That he who has the Son has life; and he that has not the Son of God has not life."

"These things have I written unto you that believe in the name of the Son of God; that you may know that you have eternal life, and that you may believe in the Name of the Son of God." 1st John 5:11-13

"Therefore, if any man be in Christ He is a new creature; Born again; old things are passed away, behold, All things are become NEW." 2Corinthians 5:17

Chapter 4

Salvation

"Vine's Dictionary says it includes deliverance, safety, preservation." (meaning health or wholeness)

Also, "conditions of repentance and faith in the Lord Jesus; in whom, Jesus, alone it is to be obtained."

Readers Digest Dictionary says, "For Salvation, means To change into another state, form, or substance; to be transformed; to change from one belief, doctrine, or course of action to another; to cause a change in character; to turn from a sinful life to a righteous life."
2Corinthians 5:17

The Word of God Agrees; "The Law of the Lord is perfect, converting the soul; the testimony of the Lord is sure, making wise the simple." Psalm 19:7

"For this people's heart is waxed gross, and their ears are dull of hearing, and their eyes they have closed; lest at any time they should see with their eyes, and hear with their ears, and should understand with their heart, and should be converted, and I should heal them." Matthew 13:15

Healing

I know healing is included in Salvation; and I want you to look at this Word in Acts 10:38.

"How God anointed Jesus of Nazareth with the Holy Ghost and with power; who went about doing good and healing all that were oppressed of the Devil; for God was with Him."

Healing and the Devil is a big clue as to who is responsible for sickness and diseases and not from God. All good things come from above.

Here are tools we can use in spiritual warfare:
In the first place, Jesus has given us the power over all the power of the Devil in Luke 10:19.

My response would be to reject the Devil and whatever he is trying to put on me, and resist it, because the Word says to, in James 4:7.

"Submit yourselves therefore to God;" That's you, resist the Devil and He will flee from you." Why would He flee? Because he is afraid of the Name of Jesus; and If you don't resist him and reject the symptoms, it means you have what you received.

"But He, Jesus, was wounded for our transgressions, He, Jesus, was bruised for our iniquities: The chastisement of our peace was upon him; and with His, Jesus, stripes we are healed." Isaiah 53:5

"That it might be fulfilled which was spoken by Eaisa's the prophet, saying, Himself, Jesus, took our infirmities, and bare our Sicknesses. Who His, Jesus, own self bare our sins in His own body on the tree, that we being dead to sins, should live unto righteousness. By whose, Jesus, tripes you were healed."

Matthew 8:17; Isaiah 53:5; 1st Peter 2:24

Deliverance

"Giving thanks unto the Father, which has made us meet, able, to be partakers of the inheritance of the saints in light; Who has delivered us from the power of darkness, and has translated us into the kingdom of His dear Son. In whom, Jesus, we have redemption through His blood, even the forgiveness of sins."

Colossians 1:12-14

Preservation and Safety

"Blessed be the God and Father of our Lord Jesus Christ, who has blessed us with all spiritual blessing in heavenly places in Christ."

Ephesians 1:3

I make scripture personal, and use the words I, me, my, instead you or your.

"A thousand shall fall at your side, and ten thousand at your right hand; but it shall not come near you . Only with your eyes shall you behold and see the reward of the wicked. Because you have made the Lord, which is your refuge, even the most High your habitation; There shall no evil befall you , neither shall any plague come nigh you're dwelling. For He shall give His Angels charge over you to keep you in all your ways. They shall bear you up in their hands, lest you dash your foot against a stone." Psalm 91 7-13

"Thy righteousness is like the great mountains; thy judgments are a great deep. O Lord, you preserve man and beast." Psalm 36:6

Soundness and Wholeness

"For God hasn't given us the spirit of fear; but of power, and of love, and of a sound mind." 2nd Timothy 1:7

"Blessed be the God and Father of our Lord Jesus Christ, who has blessed us with all spiritual blessings in heavenly places in Christ."
Ephesians 1:4

Peter speaks to a man named AEneas who was sick with palsy for eight years and says;

"AEneas, Jesus Christ makes you whole; arise, and make thy bed. And he arose immediately." Acts 9:32-34

"Peter and John went up together into the temple at the hour of prayer, and spoke to a lame man; Peter, fastening his eyes upon him with John, said, Look on us. And he gave heed unto them, expecting to receive something of them. Then Peter said, "Silver and gold have I none, but such as I have, give I thee; In the Name of Jesus Christ of Nazareth, rise up and walk." Acts 3:1-6

"And they Overcame by The Blood of the Lamb, and by the word of their testimony."

Tools:

Every believer has the tools to defeat the Devil: "In My NAME; "JESUS said, SHALL THEY CAST OUT DEVILS." That's if you choose to. Mark 16:17; Luke 10:19

You can use this verse against the Devil and say to him, "In Jesus Name I give you no place on my body, Devil." Ephesians 4:27

And in Jesus Name, and by the Blood of the Lamb and by the Grace of God, I have the authority to " bind the strongman and I break your power of all spirits of infirmity and cast you off of my body."

Come Holy Spirit and replace that which is gone. So by the "Name of Jesus and the blood of the Lamb, and by the Grace of God," it is done.! Matthew 18:18; Mark 11:13

Use the Name, the Word and the Blood, so we can say: That in the Name of Jesus and by the Blood of the Lamb and by the Grace of God, that "by His stripes I was healed," therefore by His stripes I am healed."
1st Peter 2:24

"The truth has made me free" John 8:32

For "I stand fast in the liberty wherewith Christ has made me free" from all infirmities."

Galatians 5:1

I receive my healing by the Name of Jesus; and by the Blood of the Lamb and by the Grace of God, I'm healed.

Chapter 5

Jesus Starts Speaking in Parables

It's a story about what the Kingdom of heaven is like.

"Then shall the kingdom of heaven be likened unto ten virgins, which took their lamps and went forth to meet the bridegroom. And five of them were wise, and five were foolish.

They that were foolish took their lamps, and took no oil with them: But the wise took oil in their vessels with their lamps. While the bridegroom tarried, they all slumbered and slept; And at midnight there was a cry made,

"Behold, the bridegroom comes; go ye out to meet Him." Then all those virgins arose, and trimmed their lamps; And the foolish said unto the wise Give us of your oil; for our lamps are gone out; But the wise answered saying, "Not so; lest there be not enough for us and you: but go ye rather to them that sell, and buy for yourselves."

And while they went to buy, the bridegroom came; and they that were ready went in with Him to the marriage: and the door was shut.

Afterward came also the other virgin saying, "Lord, Lord, open to us." But He answered and said, "Verily I say unto you, I know you not." Watch therefore, for you know neither the day nor the hour therein the Son of Man comes."

Matthew 25:1-13

The foolish Virgin believed, and even had a lamp and was also waiting for Jesus' return, but what did the foolish Virgin lack I asked?

Jesus responds; "The problem is the flesh, and it wars against God to be Lord, because they want their own way. That's sad because it's an everlasting decision."

Recently I was sitting in church and just before the service started, I overheard a lady sharing about a young boy who was fighting depression, and had a huge amount of guilt, and the boy took his life.

The Lord shared the following; "With God there's mercy, and there are certain conditions of a person's mind at the time of death; They either choose to take their life or they are on drugs; I save the ones on drugs; but there are consequences to taking one's life; it is that they cut themselves off from the life of Christ that was intended for them to be with God forever."

So please, don't ever take your life or you'll miss Heaven.

As far as guilt is concerned, as I was a volunteer in the prison, I remember a woman was explaining how exasperated she was because of being bombarded with guilt and just couldn't get rid of it.

We had the answer for her, there is forgiveness!

It is written in 1John 1:9, that "If we confess our sins, He is faithful and just to forgive us our sins, and to cleanse us from all unrighteousness."

That's all it takes; just ask God and He will do his part.

The work on the cross is a settled issue of guilt and shame. Thank you Jesus. When she prayed the prayer of forgiveness, you should have seen the look on her face, and how happy and relieved she was, as she began telling us that it was like a load lifted off her back. There's Always help when you ask; you will receive.

Matthew 7:7; John 14:14; Romans 10:12;Joel 2:32a; Acts 2:21; Romans 10:13

Knowing God

Do you recall that these words were spoken by Jesus himself?

"To know God, you need to spend time and attention to the Word of God and to spend time and attention to My presence."

"My Son, attend to My Words; incline your ear unto my sayings." Proverbs 4:20

"Is my hand shortened that it cannot save?" Isaiah 50:2

Whatever you are going through, go to God; Maybe you just might want to say, "You take care of it Lord and let all things go, But He'd rather you come to Him first; For He's always waiting to help. Psalm 50:15

"Draw near to God and He will draw near to you."
James 4:8; That's a promise He will keep.

"Commit your way unto the Lord; trust also in Him; and He shall bring it to pass." When you do this, you will have peace of mind. Psalm 37:5

Chapter 6

The Name of Jesus is Changeless Love

For "Jesus Christ is the same yesterday, today and forever." Hebrews 13:8

I heard this inside once, "that God's love is real and it's everlasting. Jeremiah 31:3

God also said, "God's love is not like our love; It will not fade. diminish or end, because it's an everlasting love. Psalm 102:37, John 11:6

It's the same for everyone whom He has created." We are all created in the image of God; Genesis 1:26

No matter what color, race, rich or poor, sinner or saint. God loves you and the world, because He's the same yesterday, today and forever.
Hebrews 13:8

About His faithfulness He said, "You can stake your life on it." Psalm 36:5; Psalm 89:2; Psalm 36:33; Psalm 92:1,2

It is written: "My substance was not hidden from thee, when I was made in secret and curiously wrought in the lowest parts of the earth. Your eyes did see my substance, yet being unperfect;

and in thy book all my members were written, which in continuance were fashioned, when as yet there was none of them."
Psalm 139:15,16

In summary, God wrote in a book that tells us that we were even thought of before the world began. He saw us in His minds' eye, everything about us. What we would look like; as to the shape of our face and body, the color of our eyes and hair. Even to the timing of when to be born. What an awesome God we have!.

Everlasting Love

"God so loved the world that He gave His only begotten Son, that whosoever believes in Him shall not perish but have everlasting life."
John 3:16

Just believe what He says, It's His Word. Did you notice that God is saying "that there is only one way to God?" "And that way is through His Son. John 14:6

"But God, who is rich in mercy, for His great love wherewith He loved us; Even when we were dead in sins, has quickened us together with Christ, by grace are you saved; and has raised us up together, and made us sit together in heavenly places, In Christ Jesus." Ephesians 2:4-6

"We are seated with God, which gives us the power and authority to rule and reign in this life, By one Jesus Christ." Romans 5:17

"As you have received Christ Jesus the Lord, so walk ye in Him." "Rooted and built up in Him and established in the faith."
2Corinthians 5:21

The Lord tells me this phrase often: "I see Grace and Peace flowing from the throne room of God." That's an awesome thing to hear; words like that when one is in a relationship with God.

It is written: And God said, "Let us make man in our image, after our likeness." which includes God the Father, God the Son and God the Holy Spirit, because they are One; and The Word Is Jesus. Genesis 1:26,27

"In the beginning was the WORD. Jesus is the Word, and the Word was with God, and the WORD was God." Jesus is God. "All things were made by Him and without Him was not anything made that was made." "In Him , Jesus, was life and life was the light of men." John 1:2-4

"Every spirit that confesses not that Jesus Christ has come in the flesh, is not of God This is the spirit of antichrist." 1st John 4:3

"And the Word was made flesh, and dwelt among us; and we beheld His glory; the glory as of the only begotten of the Father, full of grace and truth." John 1:14

My first encounter with God was in 1974; this is the Word which I heard verbally out of the sky, next to a Lake. No one was around to hear it, but it was so loud that I thought the whole world heard it. The loud voice came from Heaven and said, "Be still and know that I am God."

God made himself known to me, but it didn't register in my mind or my spirit until later in life, that Jesus is God. Psalm 46:10 Back then I was too busy raising four children. Now I'm beginning to be hungry for more of the God who spoke to me years ago.

"Believe you not, that I am in the Father and the Father in Me?

41

(Jesus' prayer to the Father) "That they all may be One; as you, Father, are in Me, and I in you, that they also may be One in us; that the world may believe that you have sent me."
John 17:21

Chapter 7

It is written

———

"And the Lord God formed man of the dust of the ground and breathed into his nostrils the breath of life, which was everlasting life; the breath of life which includes a seed."

"And the Lord God took the man and put him into the garden to dress it and to keep; and the Lord God commanded the man saying, of every tree of the garden you may freely eat; but of the tree of knowledge of good and evil, you shall not eat of it; for in the day you eat of it, you shall surely die."

"Then the Lord God said, "it isn't good that the man be alone; I will make him a helpmeet for him." And the Lord God Caused a deep sleep to fall upon Adam as he Slept; and He Took one of his ribs and closed up the FLESH; and the rib which the Lord God had taken from man, made He a woman and brought Her unto the man."

"And they were both naked, the man and his wife, and were not ashamed."
Genesis 2:7,8,15,17,21,24

"Now the birth of Jesus Christ was on this wise;" (way)

"When His mother, Mary, was espoused to Joseph, an Angel was sent to Mary at Nazareth." "And the Angel said unto her, "Fear not Mary; for you have found favor with; God and behold, you shall conceive in your womb and bring forth a son and shall call His name Jesus. "

"He shall be great and shall be called the Son of the Highest; and the Lord God shall give unto Him the throne of his father David; And He shall reign over the house of Jacob forever; and of His kingdom there shall be no end."

(I believe that God also caused Mary to receive the seed of life in the same way; in a deep sleep)

"Then said Mary unto the Angel," "How shall this be, seeing I know not a man?" And Angel answered and said unto her, "the Holy Ghost shall come upon you, and the power of the highest shall overshadow you In a deep sleep."

"Therefore also, that Holy thing, a seed, which shall be born of you shall be called the Son of God. And Mary said, Behold the handmaid of the Lord; be it unto me according to thy Word. And the Angel departed from her." Matthew 1:18-25

Jesus says, "I am the way, the truth and the life: no man comes unto the Father but by Me." John 14:6

"I AM the Door of the sheep." John 14:6

"The thief comes not, but for to steal, and to kill, and to destroy: I am come that they might have life, and that they might have it more abundantly."

"I AM the good shepherd: the good shepherd gives His life for the sheep; But he who is an hireling, and not the shepherd, whose own the sheep are not, sees the wolf coming, and leaves the sheep and flees: and the wolf catches them and scatters them. The hireling flees because he is an hierling and cares not for the sheep."

"I AM The Good Shepherd and know my sheep, and am known of mine." John 10:10-14

"And I give unto them eternal life; and they shall never perish,neither shall any man pluck them out of My hand." John 10:28

The Name of Jesus

People have written a whole book on the Name of Jesus. God help me now to share that which is pleasing in your sight.

The one thing that I have learned that is important to me, is that there's power in that Name; together with the Blood and His Word, as I have victory every time over the Devil.

Jesus said, "Behold, I give unto you power to tread on serpents and scorpions, and over all the power of the enemy and nothing shall by any means hurt you."

"And these signs shall follow them that believe; In My Name shall they cast out devils, they shall speak with new tongues; they shall lay hands on the sick and they shall recover." Luke 10:19

"And they overcame him, the Devil, by the Blood of the Lamb and by the Word of their testimony." Revelation 12:11

Does that sound like a defeated church? There's power in the blood!

"That at the Name of Jesus every knee should bow; of things in heaven, and things in earth, and things under the earth." Philippians 2:10

This is John speaking:

"And I saw heaven opened, and behold a white horse; and He sat upon him was called Faithful and True, and in righteousness He doth judge and make war. His eyes were as a flame of fire, and on His head were many crowns; and he had a name written, that no man knew, but He, Jesus, himself. And He was clothed with a vesture dipped in blood: and his name is called The Word of God." Revelation 19:11-13

"I Am Alpha and Omega, the beginning and the ending, says the Lord; which is, which was, and which is to come. "I am He that lives and was dead; which is and which was, and which is to come, the Almighty." Revelation 1:8

"And this is the record that God has given to us eternal life, and this life is in His Son. He that has the Son has life; and he who has not the Son of God has not life. These things have I written unto you that believe on the Name of the Son of God, that you may know that you have eternal life; and that you may believe on the Name of the Son of God." 1st John 5:11-13

Chapter 8

Conditions to follow Jesus

SELFLESSNESS, and HOLINESS

Follow peace with all men, and holiness, without which no man shall see the Lord.

Looking diligently lest any man fail of the grace of God; lest any root of bitterness springing up trouble you, and thereby many be defiled. Hebrews 12:14:

"It's the pure in heart that will see God." Matthew 5:8

"Because you are free from sin, your fruit will be Holy and the free gift is Eternal Life." Romans 6:22

"God Talked about having faith, love and Holiness with sobriety. Choosing to be sober so that it goes well with you, and see many good days." 1Thessilonians 5:6

"For I say, Paul, through the grace given unto me, to every man that is among you, not to think of himself more highly than he ought to think; but to have a sober mind according as God has dealt to every man the measure of faith." Romans 12:3

There will always be consequences for bad choices; and good rewards for good and wise choices.

Having His Mind in All Things

"God will chasten or discipline us to bring about holiness, but just as He has told us, "the blessings far outweigh the disciplines that are required of you." The Holy Spirit will teach us how to be selfless. Hebrews 12:10

I have learned that in order to be filled with the Holy Spirit, one needs to ask Jesus to Baptize you in the Holy Ghost; for Jesus is the Baptizer. John 1:33

And to continue to be filled, is to empty yourself out and drink in the Holy Spirit.

Selflessness

And His mind in All things

"I beseech you, therefore brethren, by the mercies of God, that you present your bodies a living sacrifice, holy unto God; which is your reasonable service; And be not conformed to this world: but be ye transformed by the renewing of your mind; that you may prove what is that good , and acceptable, and perfect will of God."

"For I say, through the Grace given unto me, to every man who is among you , not to think of himself more highly than he ought to think; but to think soberly , according as God has dealt to every man the measure of faith." Romans 12:1-3

However, it is a total surrender to God and His Lordship to do His perfect will. it's our responsibility to find out just what purpose He has for us, using our spiritual gifts. It's an ongoing

CONDITIONS TO FOLLOW JESUS

process to mature, and to become more Christ like, with an ongoing relationship; But the New Birth is instantaneous.

Now you need to know that first: you are spirit, then you have a soul, which is made up of three parts; It's your mind, will and emotions; and you live in a body. Your spirit is the real you. Your SPIRIT never dies. It's a serious decision you have to make because that's forever; and the choice is choosing Lordship. See how important this is? 3John 2

"Yes, you have a free will, Jesus has said ; and it's a choice to whom you belong and where to spend eternal life."

Chapter 9

"Words from the Lord for You"

"Number 1."

H e said; "Sin is covered up these days. It's neither white nor black. It's sort of in the middle except it's like it's not so bad; everybody is doing it anyway. Why not go all the way. Do just anything you want to do. Let it all hang out. Sort of loose, you know what I mean?

To Me it's something I will not tolerate. How can I be Holy and sinful at the same time; It just doesn't work that way. Pure is pure and sin is sinful.

The grace that I have can change all of it; from the very worst to the very best.

Beloved, I wish above all things that you prosper and be in good health, just as your soul prospers I want the very best for everyone."

Psalm 23; John 7:37,38,39; Isaiah 55:3; Revelation 22:17
1John 1:9; 3John 2; James 4:17; Hebrews 13:5

Holiness and Selflessness

"Number 2"

"Conditions to follow Jesus is Holiness; for which you cannot see God; and to have the mind of Christ in all things. To Me; honor is due to My Holy Name. The One True God who is worthy of all your praise; "I Am Alpha and Omega, the beginning and the ending. The Most High and lifted up." Revelation 1:8

"Surely goodness and mercy shall follow you all the days of your life;" is My promise to those who choose to follow Me and be My disciple. No one greater in My Kingdom is than this, the one who chooses to be My child; for they will be a little lower than the angels.

Truth is found in My Word. Search for it. Look for it like fine treasures of gold. Be hungering and thirsting and you shall be filled and satisfied."

Psalm 23; John 7:37,38,39; Isaiah 55:3; Revelation 22:17; Hebrews 13:5

"Number3"

"To you; everything you will ever need is supplied by Me, In My Name.

You have not? Maybe it's because you haven't asked the Father in heaven in My Name; He will do it. Have faith that you have it and believe in Me."

Grace isn't cheap. It came by paying a great price, for which I was more than willing to do, to sacrifice MY life for yours. Just think. No one was the perfect sacrifice. No greater than I can say This."

Ephesians 1:7,8; Isaiah 1:18; Hebrews 8:12; 1Peter 3:10-12; 1Thesselonians 4:17; Matthew 5:8; Romans 6:22; 1Timothy 2:13-15;2; Corinthians 7:1; 1stTimothy 2:13-15; Hebrews 12:10; Isaiah 41:10; John 15:16b

"Number 4"

"The Blessings far outweigh the disciplines that are required of thee. Excitement, surprises and intrigue will be the norm. Not dull does and don'ts.

The love that I have removes all doubts and fears, which Satan will try to tempt you with. It's never from Me, but it should draw you closer and not farther away.

So Grace is the Key Word; because it will only be by My Grace that you will be able to do this. My love sustains and strengthens. It never diminishes or weakens. It's always there. My love never fails. Remember that.

So look unto Me, the rock from which you were hewed. Walking worthily with Me; "for I will never leave you nor forsake you;" and faithfulness will never fail."

1John 1:9; 3rdJohn 2; James 4:17; Isaiah 51:1

His Mind In All Things

"Cleanse yourselves of the flesh and of the spirit." 2nd Corinthians 7:12

When the Bible speaks of the flesh, it mostly means our soul, and not our physical body. Remember I told you that the soul is our mind, will and emotions; well your soul doesn't get transformed like your spirit does when you are saved. It's your spirit that gets born again, or changed.

I recall an evangelist who gave the interpretation of "being born again;" it's the divine exchange from our sinful nature into God's Holy nature; the very nature of Jesus; as well as changing Lordship, from Satan to Jesus.

It is written, "If any man be in Christ, he is a New creature. Old things pass away and behold all things become new." 2nd Corinthians 5:17

Let's see what it means to cleanse our Soul. Remember that the SOUL is your MIND, will , and EMOTIONS. Let's start with the first part of your soul, the MIND: "Jesus reminded us that we need the mind of Christ in all things." Philippians 3:16

"Be not conformed to this world, but be transformed by the renewing of your mind; that you may prove what is that good and acceptable, perfect will of God." Romans 12:2

How do we renew our minds? "By the Word of God;" Reading it and meditating on the truth of God's Word. The longer we are in the Word, the more truth we know and the truth is what sets us free. Ephesians 4:23

Our Will: I believe it's all by surrendering your will to the will of God in ALL things. Actually, it's surrendering your will to the Lordship of Jesus Christ rather than from the Lordship of Satan, which we Inherited; passed down what the Devil did in the Garden of Eden which made him our Lord and ruled us.

When you open the door of your heart, you actually want Him to come inside of you to change your spirit into a New Spirit of His life.

It's actually choosing where you will spend everlasting life; in heaven or hell. And He won't force you either, It's your choice.

Is their room in your heart for Jesus? "Just invite Him in and ask Jesus to be Lord of your life." Revelation 3:20

Just think; if Adam and Eve didn't eat of the Tree of Good and Evil, they would have lived forever, and so would we. However, because they did eat of the tree and were tempted by the Devil, Lucifer, they both became aware that they were naked.

That's when they hid because they felt guilty. Don't we feel the same uncomfortable feeling of guilt when we sin?

So what did God say if they did eat? "they would die." God made them leave the garden and became separated from God; SIN SEPARATES us FROM GOD, and from then on, death ruled them and us..

Genesis 2:15-25; Genesis 3:9-24

Do you know who the Devil is? He is also called Satan and Lucifer. He was the most beautiful of Angels in heaven, and he had so much pride that he even wanted to be God himself, and have God worship him.

"Jesus said, I saw him fall from heaven like lightning; him and his angels." Luke 10:18

I know some people are afraid to die, but it shouldn't be if you knew God, through Jesus.

Oh how He loves us and would tell you often too; He is so loving, kind and merciful. He's just waiting for you to come as you are.

He loves those whom He created, and that's the whole world too. 1stJohn4:18 and John 3:16

He's not stingy and He proved that He loves you because He came down in the flesh to take upon Himself your sin and mine and for the whole world. No wonder "He cried out on the cross, "My God, My God, why have you forsaken Me." Matthew 27:46

God separates Himself from sinners, even His own Son, and you will not find sin or sinners in heaven; But God was merciful to all; even towards His Son Genesis 3; Matthew 27:46

So we were on the Cross with Him; therefore, we were with Him in Hell.

"God strengthened Him and took the keys of death and Hell; and made a show of him openly." That means He paraded the Devil in front of his cohorts and took the keys of Hell and death, and triumphed over him." Revelation 1:18

God not only raised Jesus, but raised us up along with Him." Ephesians 2:4-6

If you have never heard this before, let me share it again with you.

Then on the 3rd day "God raised us up together to sit with God; with authority, to reign in life by one Jesus Christ." Ephesians2:6

"Jesus died for us, He didn't need to, we did. He did it for us. That means we were there with Him and Triumphed with Him. Here we were, complete in Him; as it says in the Word, "Know you not, that so many of us were baptized into Jesus Christ were baptized into His death." Romans 6:4

"Therefore we were buried with Him by Baptism into death." Yes; but more than that, we were raised up together with Him; Ephesians 2:6

"That like Christ was raised up from the dead by the glory of the Father, even so we should walk in newness of life. Romans 6:4

"But now being made free; and redeemed from the curse of the LAW of sin and death; from sin, and becoming servants to God; you have your fruit unto Holiness and the end everlasting life; Romans 8:2

"But the gift of God is eternal life through Jesus Christ our Lord." "For the wages of sin is death." Romans 6:22,23

Our Emotions

The Word of God says that "we need to cleanse our flesh and spirit."

That's for sure, because offenses will show up, and it's good not to have anything between you and your God. That's called unforgiveness. Matthew 6:14, 15

So let's deal with Cleansing of the flesh.

Now then even after we are saved, you need to know this; that there is a war going on inside of us. "That the lust of the flesh is against the Spirit, and the Spirit is against the flesh." But if you are led by the Spirit, you are not under the LAW" "For to be carnally minded is death; but to be spiritually minded is life and peace."

Too long has our minds dominated over our spirit; and They that are in the flesh cannot please God." Galatians 5:17,18

What then are the works of the flesh?

Works of the flesh

Galatians 5:19-26

"Adultery, fornication, uncleanness, lasciviousness; when I see a big word like this I looked it up in the Vine's Dictionary; and it means having a manifestation or arousing sensual desire.

20. Idolatry, witchcraft, hatred, variance, emulations, wrath, strife, seditions, heresies,

21. Envyings murders, drunkenness, revellings, and such like: of the which I tell you before, as I have also in time past, "that they which do such things shall not inherit the kingdom of God. Galatians 5:19-21

22. "But the fruit of the Spirit is love, joy, peace, long suffering, gentleness, goodness, faith.

23. Meekness, temperance: against such there is no law.

24. And they that are Christ's have crucified the flesh with the affections and lusts.

25. If we live in the Spirit let us also walk in the Spirit.

26. Let us not be deciduous of vain glory, provoking one another, enveying one another." Galatians 5:22-26

So truly a turning away from these things is from the heart; It means repentance with an honest confession, once and forever.

For years we have been ruled by Satan and going the ways of the world. We have been programmed by wrong thinking, reasoning things out, or going by our senses: in how we feel, instead of finding out what the Word of God has to say.

There's a Word for every situation.

Through the power of the Holy Spirit, together with a renewed mind and by the truth of the Word of God, we will have victory in every area of our life.

Next: Cleanse our spirit

Galatians 6:7-10
"Be not deceived; God is not mocked; for whatsoever a man soweth that shall he also reap."

8. "For he that soweth to his flesh shall of the flesh reap corruption; but he that soweth to the Spirit shall of the Spirit reap life everlasting. "

9. "And let us not be weary in well doing' for in due season we shall reap, if we faint not."

10. "As we have therefore opportunity, let us do good unto all men, especially unto them who are of the household of faith."

Jesus said, "See how important the Word is to us? "For It is the Spirit that quickens, makes life; the flesh profits nothing; the Word which I have spoken unto you, they are Spirit and they are life." John 6:63

"Man does not live by bread alone, but by every Word that proceeds out of the mouth of God." Matthew 4:4

Did you know that the Bible tells us, "that the Word of God is life and health to all our flesh?" 3 rd John 2

The Word of God says we need to feed on the Word, as it is like spiritual Food." It's just like medicine, to nourish our bodies.

Have you ever thought of the Word as Life? Let that sink in because it's saying,

"Our life depends on it;" and another way God put it, It's Our very life is dependent on God's Love.

That covers all of our spirit, soul and our body. What an awesome God we have! There's one more thing I could add:

It says in God's Word, Jesus says, "Now are you clean through the Word which I have spoken unto you. They are Spirit and they are life." John 6:63

Have you ever thought that reading the Bible makes you clean? John 15:3;

As it also says; we become clean by "the washing of water by the Word." Ephesians 5:26;

Keep that in mind when the next time you read the Words Of God. Agree?

It's the Spirit of the WORD of God that makes it alive; it's like water that washes us,

Water? Yes, God knows how we are when we feel guilty; Does the Devil make you feel dirty sometimes? He's good at putting you under, if he could.

Here is what Jesus said that we need!

Jesus said "My people are destroyed for lack of knowledge." Whose against us? but the Devil and our fleshly mind. We need to hear words of Truth, instead of lies, because the Devil is a liar and the Father of it." John 8:44

Chapter 10

The New Covenant of My Blood

Under the Old Covenant, the sacrificing of animals was just a covering for the peoples' sins.

"Under the New Covenant was the shedding of the precious blood of Jesus, which cleansed our sins; pacifying the guilty conscience." "There is therefore now no condemnation to those who are in Christ Jesus."

The Christian is freed from a guilty conscience.

"Now the God of Peace that brought again from the dead our Lord Jesus; That Great Shepherd of the sheep through the blood of the everlasting covenant."

"And almost all things are by law purged with blood; and without shedding of blood is no remission." "My Covenant will I not break, nor alter the thing that is gone out of My lips." "

In whom, Jesus, we have redemption through His Blood, even the forgiveness of our sins."

Romans 8:1;Hebrews 13:20; Hebrews 9:22; Psalm 89:34; Colossians 1:14

"A Word from the Lord"

"I AM A COVENANT KEEPING GOD:"

"If you receive Me into your heart, you are sealed together with Me forever. I will not fail you nor forsake you. When you do this, I will engrave you in the palm of My hand and your face will be forever before Me.

This covenant I will not break nor alter the thing that has gone out of My lips, just like My servant Donna has told you.

Be brave in the face of adversities for I Am the Lord, The Great I Am! I am all that you need pertaining to life and godliness.

Is My hand shortened that it cannot save? No! A hundred times No! I say. Believe and it shall be so to you. For I have called you this day to surrender to Me all that disturbs and concerns you. My ear isn't too heavy to hear either.

I will be God to you, if you make Me Lord of Your Life."

Psalm 89:34; Hebrews 13:5; Psalm 89; Isaiah 50:2; 1Peter 5:7; Isaiah 59:1

The Power of the Blood

Jesus' sacrificed His life to set us free on the Cross: Not the blood of animals that just COVERED the sins of the people, but by the precious blood of Jesus; satisfying the LAW and the debt we owe. "For the wages of sin is death."

Jesus' Victory over Satan was for us: "And having spoiled principalities and power. He, "Jesus, made a show openly, means He Paraded him in front of his cohorts, triumphing over them in it."

Jesus said, "I am the Resurrection and the life." "Then God raised us up together to sit with Him in heavenly places, reigning in this life by One Jesus Christ."

There's Power in the NAME. Mark 16:17
There's Power in the BLOOD. Revelation 12:11
There's power in the WORD. Hebrews 4:12
We have whatsoever we say. Mark 11:23
"Now thanks be to God which always causes us to triumph in Christ." Romans 6:23:
Colossians 2:15; Romans 5:17; John 11:26

"A Word from the Lord"

"This is Essential to know that there's power in the Blood."

It is written "And they overcame Him, the Devil, by the Blood of the Lamb and by the word of their testimony." Revelation 12:11

I want to take you way back in history to the days of Moses. "God has sent him to deliver the Israelites from bondage from King Pharaoh, and after many plagues were demonstrated, He continued to disobey God.

God then said that He would destroy the first born male, because of his disobedience and to set the Israelites free. "For I will pass through the land of Egypt this night, and will emit all first born in the land of Egypt; both men and beast and against all the gods of Egypt.

I will execute judgment. And the blood shall be to you a token upon the houses where you are; and when I see the blood,

I will pass over you and the plague shall not be upon you, when I smite the land of Egypt And you shall take a bunch of hyssop and dip it in the blood that is in the basin, and strike the lintel and the two side posts with the blood that is in the basin; and none of you shall go out at the door of his house until morning."
Exodus 12:12,22

The Passover

"For the Lord will pass through to smite the Egyptians; and when I see the blood upon the mantel and on the two side posts, the Lord will pass over the door, and will not allow the destroyer to come unto your house to smite you."

"And you shall observe this thing for an ordinance to you and to your sons forever."
Exodus 12:23,24

My thoughts;

I believe in the power of the BLOOD of Jesus; and from this example of applying the BLOOD by faith on the doorposts of a house for protection, I have chosen to do the same in our Condo by faith, and the same for our households houses as well.

Chapter 11

Our New Position in Christ

Does that sound like we are beneath and under the thumb of the Devil? Hardly! We have a new position in Christ with authority, yes, and "power over all the power of the enemy." and it's time for you and the Church to know it and to live it." Luke 10:19:

"Giving thanks unto the Father, which has made us to be partakers of the inheritance of the saints in light; Who has delivered us from the power of darkness and has translated us into the kingdom of his dear Son." Colossians 1:12-13

For this reason, Satan doesn't have the right to rule or dominate Christians now.

Yes, Satan is running things now, but we are not of the world, we are in the world. Our citizenship is in heaven.

Jesus said, "Behold, I give unto you power to tread on serpents and scorpions, and over all the power of the enemy; and nothing (nothing, nothing) shall by any means hurt you." Luke 10:19

These truths need to be built on in our lives until it becomes a part of us, and exercised in the church today.

The problems that exist are because we permit them. We're the ones who are supposed to do something about them; using our authority that was given us. Ephesians 1:21-23

Jesus is the Greater One

"Greater than he that is in us, than he that is in the world." 1John 4:4

We have the power over demons, evil spirits, sickness and diseases; For Jesus said, "Behold, I give unto you power over serpents and scorpions, and over ALL the power of the enemy, and nothing by any means shall hurt you." Luke 10:19

And they overcame him by the Blood of the Lamb, and by the word of their testimony." Revelation 12:11

You must Believe who you are in Christ, and that His power is our power. It is written: "We are More than Conquerors through Him, Jesus, who loved us." Romans 8:37

"I have whatsoever I say. " Mark 11:23

Whatever circumstance we have; no matter what symptom we have on our body, we should always stand fast in the Liberty wherewith Christ has made us free! " Galatians 5:1

Lest we forget! It is written, "He, Jesus, having spoiled principalities and powers, He, Jesus, made a show of them openly, triumphing over them in it." Colossians 2:15

"Jesus paraded the Devil in Hell and all his cohorts and took the keys of death and hell from the Devil." Revelation 1:18

Because we are spirit, the real you will miss the grave and will go straight to heaven when we die, if one chooses Jesus as Lord and Savior.

Jesus said, "I Am He that lives and was dead; and behold, I live for evermore." Revelation 1:18

It is written, Jesus says to Peter; "Upon this rock I will build My Church, and the gates of Hell shall not prevail against it; and I will give unto you the keys of the kingdom of heaven; and whatsoever you shall bind on earth shall be bound in heaven; and whatsoever you shall loose on earth shall be loosed from heaven." "But first Bind the Strong man, then you can spoil his goods."

Matthew 16:18,19; Matthew 12:29;
Ephesians 2:4-6

Knowledge or No Knowledge

Jesus gave this illustration of a wise man and a foolish man.

"Therefore, whosoever heareth these sayings of mine, and does them, I will liken him unto a wise man, which built his house upon a rock. And the rain descended, and the floods came, and the winds blew, and beat upon that house; and it fell not; for it was founded upon a rock."

And everyone that heareth these sayings of mine, and does them not, shall be likened unto a foolish man, which built his house upon the sand; And the rain descended, and the floods came, and the winds blew, and beat upon that house; and it fel: and great was the fall of it." Matthew 7:24-27

"But be ye doers of the Word and not hearers only, deceiving your souls." James 1:22

We need to be wise and not foolish in how we build our foundation; it must be grounded on the Word of God. Especially now, during times of uncertainty of our Nation, and things to come.

God's love won't fail us nor forsake us; and of His faithfulness we can have peace, no matter what comes. It is the faithfulness of His love that grounds us. Do you know Him that well? Hebrews 13:5

"A Word from the Lord"

> "It's imperative that you know how to back
> yourself up in the Word."

Back Up Scriptures

for SATANS' ACCUSATIONS:

If Satan -

1. "Reminds you of your past and you feel guilty, "Say, In 1st John 1:9 says, "I am forgiven if I confessed my sins," I did, so I Am forgiven.

2. "What makes you think You're not Saved?

In John 3:16 says, "If I believe in Jesus, so I am

3. "You're going to die early in life.

Say, "It is not for you to know the times or the seasons which God the Father is the only one who knows. You're a liar; get out in Jesus Name. Acts 1:7

4. If Satan Gives you trouble, like an anxiety attack: Say: "In Jesus Name," Get out of here." He's afraid of that NAME.

5. Don't let yourself be afraid, when we have God on our side. Psalm 118:6

Say, "No weapon formed against me shall prosper." Jesus is Lord. Isaiah 54:17; Matthew 16:18

6. When Satan overwhelms you with cares, like carrying a heavy load.

"Cast ALL your care upon the Lord and He shall sustain you." Psalm 55:22

If Satan threatens you-

7. Satan the accuser haunts you. "There is therefore now no condemnation to them which are, in Christ Jesus, who walk not after the flesh, but after the Spirit." Romans 8:1

8. When Satan causes you to doubt, "The gates of hell shall not prevail against me." Matthew 16:18

9. "I choose to walk by faith and not by sight." 2Corinthians 5:17

10. When Satan brings feelings that you're not loved; Remind him and yourself, "that God loves you as much as He loves Jesus." John 17:23

"A Word from the Lord "

"The Word has lost its power, only when it is unspoken."

"So when fear, doubt and unbelief comes on you, Say: "In the Name of Jesus, I bring into captivity every thought to the obedience of Christ." 2nd Corinthians 10:5

WORDS to SAY: "For the LAW of the Spirit of Life in Christ Jesus has made me free from the Law of sin and death." Romans 8:2

"Quote the Word; the Lord Jesus has made me free from the Law of sin and death.

"No weapon formed against me, shall prosper." Isaiah 54:17

"I am persuaded that neither death, nor life, nor principalities, nor powers, nor things present, nor things to come shall be able to separate me from the love of God, which is in Christ Jesus." Romans 8:38,39

"As the mountains are about Jerusalem, so the Lord God is around His people now and even for ever." Psalm 125:2

Chapter 12

"Cover your Head with the Word"

It is written: "Put on the whole armor of God; the girdle of truth, the breastplate of righteousness, shod your feet with the Gospel of peace, the shield of Faith, to quench the fiery darts of the wicked, the Helmet of Salvation, and the sword of the Spirit (which is the Word of God." Ephesians 6:13-17

No weapon formed against you shall prosper; and every tongue that shall arise against you in judgment, you shall condemn, This is the heritage of the servants of the Lord, and their righteousness is of Me, saith the Lord."
Isaiah 54:17

"God didn't give you the spirit of Fear, but of power, love and of a sound mind." 2nd Timothy 1:7

"In the Name of Jesus, I Give (you) no place on my body."
Ephesians 4:27

"Christ has redeemed you from the curse of the Law".
Galatians 3:13

"The thoughts that I have towards you are thoughts of peace and not of evil."
Jeremiah 29:11

If my thoughts are not peaceful, it's the enemy.

"The Lord is my keeper." "The Lord shall preserve your going out and your coming in from this time forth, and even for evermore."
Psalm 121:5,8

"This one is for the CORONAVIRUS; "There shall no evil befall you, me, neither shall any plague come nigh your, my, dwelling. For He has given His Angels charge over you, me, to keep you me, in all your ways, my, ways." Psalm 91:10, 11

"For He shall give His Angels charge over you, me, to keep me in all my ways." Psalm 91:11

"The Lord shall preserve my going out and coming in, from this time forth, and forever more." Psalm 121:8

God has chosen 15 verses for me to read every morning; so out of obedience that's what I do on a daily basis; So after reading them so many times, I have learned them and say the following 15 verses:

1. Curses of the LAW are; "Curses of sickness and diseases."' Deuteronomy 28:15 and below.

2. "But if you do get sick, Jesus said, "For I am the Lord who heals you." Exodus 15:26

3. "And you shall serve the Lord your God, and He shall bless your bread and your water; and He shall take sickness away from the midst of thee. Your young shall not be barren in your land and the number of your days I will fulfill." Exodus 23:24-26

4. "There shall no evil befall you, neither shall any plague come nigh your dwelling; For He shall give His Angels

charge over you to keep you in all of your ways." Psalm 91:10 & 11

5. "Bless the Lord, Oh my soul; and all that is within me, bless His Holy Name." "Bless the Lord Oh my soul and forget not ALL His benefits: who forgives all thine, my, iniquities; who heals ALL thy, my, diseases." Psalm 103:2&3

6. "So shall My Word be that goes forth out of My mouth, it shall not return unto Me void; it shall accomplish that which I please and prosper in the thing whereto I sent it." Isaiah 55:11

7. "Jesus said of Himself, I came not to do My own will, but the will of Him that sent Me." "How God has anointed Jesus of Nazareth with the Holy Ghost and with power; who went about doing good and healing all that were oppressed of the Devil; For God was with Him." Acts 10:38

8. "Then Jesus said to His disciples, "Go ye into the world and preach the gospel to every creature. And these signs shall follow them that believe; In My Name shall they cast out devils; they shall lay hands on the sick and they shall recover." Mark 16:15, 17, 18

9. "Is there any sick among you? Let him call for the elders of the church; and let them pray over him, anointing him with oil in the Name of the Lord: and the prayer of faith shall save the sick, and the Lord shall raise him up; and if he has committed any sins, they shall be forgiven him." James 5:14, 15

10. "Beloved; I wish above all things that you prosper and be in good health, even as your soul prosper. 3ʳᵈ John:2

11. "Jesus Christ is the same, yesterday, today and forever." Hebrews 13:8

12. "'Jesus said, I would never leave you nor forsake you." Hebrews 13:5

13. "You are of God, little children: and have overcome them: because greater is He that is he that is in you, than he that is in the world." 1st John 4:4

14. "For verily I say unto you, that whosoever shall say to this mountain; Be thou removed and be cast into the sea; and shall not doubt in his heart, but shall believe that those things which he says shall come to pass; he shall have whatsoever he says." Mark 11:23

And when I read that verse, I said Lord, "that sounds like positive thinking?" And the Lord answered, "You may call it that, but it is true!"

15. "Therefore I say unto you, what things whatsoever you desire, when you pray, believe that you receive them and you shall have them."

Mark 11:24

16. "Thou openest thy hand, and satisfiest the desire of every living thing." Psalm 145:16

Chapter 13

Going Deeper

"Deep Calls unto Deep;" How deep do you want to go with God?"

This was the phrase Jesus used in the "Course On Love;" So God wants you to know "Do you Know Me?" "You can, through Jesus."

Do you seek Me?

"But seek ye first the kingdom of God and His righteousness; and all these things shall be added unto you." Matthew 6:33

Do you Call on Me?

"Then shall you call upon Me, and you shall go and pray unto Me, and I hearken unto you."

Is it from your mind or your heart?

"And you shall seek Me, and find Me, when you shall search for Me with all of your heart."

"And I will be found of you, saith the Lord." Jeremiah 29:12-14.

If you want to know Jesus and have the Knowledge of Jesus? Start reading the Book of John. And to know what Christ is saying to you, the Church; read the Epistles of Paul; starting at Romans and end with Revelation.

If you're a hungry believer, and want more of Jesus, just ask Him to Baptize you with His Holy Spirit. Then you'll grow deeper spiritually.

Jesus' concern for His people, was that they are destroyed for lack of knowledge. (His People are everyone who He has created),

Because you have rejected knowledge, I will also reject you, that thou will be no priest to Me: seeing you have forgotten the Law (the Word) of your God, I will also forget your children. Hosea 4:6

For me, my foundation was built upon from my youth, and my parents brought me to Church; called Sunday School from a very young age. That alone tells you where you and your children need the foundation of truth; just as the Word of God says, "Train up a child in the way he should go, and when he is old, he will not depart from it." Proverbs 22:6

Not only that, but a child's parents are an umbrella of protection, in a spiritual way. It's an atmosphere of love and respect for each other, yes, with limits and boundaries. Or we'll have a lawless generation. It would be a stable life for sure when life around you falls apart.

We have a faithful God; Believe what He says in the Bible, which are the words of God speaking to us and you personally. In fact, there is a verse for every situation you will ever have, is there for you to uncover for help from above.

When I was in my teens someone said to me, "God didn't promise you a bed of roses, but God promises He'll never fail you, nor forsake you, and is saying to you as He said to me;

"Fear not; for I am with you: be not dismayed, for I am your God; I will strengthen you; yea, I will help you; yea, and I will uphold you with the right hand of my righteousness." Hebrews 13:5; Isaiah 41:10

When growing up, just what did your eyes see, and what did your ears hear as you grew up;

It's very important to keep yourself and your children in a safe place. This is a good reminder even for spiritually mature adults. If we want to please God, watch what you see, hear and where you go.

Now that you are older, are you still missing something in your life? Do you feel an emptiness inside?

You know, there's a special place within you that is meant for God alone; remember God created you, didn't He?

Listen now to the word of the Lord for you. " I wish that all my children would come to Me, that I may give them the abundant life that I have promised." This isn't hard to do, to go to God who loves you.

All of God's children, young and old, are precious in His sight.

The Word of God says that we were made in the image of God before the foundation of the world.

He wrote in a book all your members; what you would look like, the color of your eyes, the color of your hair and yes, your shape. Psalm 139:14-16

You are not your own. You were bought with a price. The Blood of Jesus. So the question is then, to whom do you belong?

Satan rules us, believe it not; So he has the right to claim you because of the disobedience to God by Adam and Eve;

However, God gives You a free will to choose to whom you belong.

God said in His teaching that "You have a free will to choose to whom you will obey, and He said, "it was an everlasting decision.

I heard that God loves me from my youth, but I didn't know that He loves me just as much as He loves Jesus; I found that out in my old age. I discovered it myself; just by reading the Bible, in John 17:23

What an eye opener to learn how much we are loved by God. His love is so great, that He sent His only Son to die in our place on the cross. God showed us just how much He loves us by making our sins as white as snow; just as if we never sinned. Isaiah 1:18; Psalm 51:7

Recently the Lord shared this: "I called you when you were young. Now that you are old, I will never abandon you nor forsake you."

Isn't that neat! It was a desire God put into my heart and He drew me to Jesus and God Himself; to love them both with all of my heart; and yes obey Him; for we are One.

It's a seeking heart that will find Him; and it's a promise in the Word, "For those who shall call upon Me, and go and pray to Me, I will answer you. You shall seek Me and find Me, when you search for Me with all of your heart; And I will be found of you, says the Lord." Jeremiah 29:12-14

One has to be hungry to go Deeper, that was what I was. I went to a Pastor to find God, and I asked him to pray that I might Meet the God that spoke to me so many years ago; And when he did, I was immediately filled with His presence. Talk about peaceful and so comfortable, I was like a babe in His arms, and slowly just laid on the floor.

Oh yes, Jesus is real.

Chapter 14

Jesus said;
"Closeness is a Relationship"

~~~

That quote from the Lord, means; one needs to talk to Him and have a relationship with Him; and when you hear his voice, you can question it, because Satan is a counterfeit. Just ask Jesus, did you say that? Or, Jesus please confirm what I heard.

"In The Name of Jesus" It is written; "And these signs shall follow them that believe." Are you a believer? Jesus himself said it in Mark 16:17.

To me that sounds like delegated power.

Since I received the Baptism of the Holy Spirit, I was under the attack of the devil daily; he was trying to take over my body to control me.

I have learned that the Lord's presence is warm and comfortable, but the devil's presence is hot with pressure. So we learn the differences. The believer will be challenged. But, All good things come from above. Know that! Know the difference. The good from the bad.

All good things comes from above, If it's bad, then you need to know what to do about it and use the Name and the Word of

God. Beware of symptoms also, if they are good or bad. You'll know right away after being used for a while.

Do you remember
The movie, "The Wizard of OZ."
Where Judy Garland is running in the field joyfully singing on the way to see the Wizard? When suddenly she becomes very, very sleepy; so much so she said, "I have to stop!

I feel so sleepy, I got to lie down?

In the movie, Glenda the Good Witch comes to rescue her; Likewise, those who know about spiritual matters, know what's going on. The sleepy symptom is Satan's Work, and can be overcome in the Name of Jesus. Judy needed help. If you need help like this, call on Jesus, He will deliver you. John 2:21

SATAN'S WORK

The Devil and familiar spirits know all about us; and the Devil also knows scripture better than you do, and can quote them and sound like Jesus himself, and you'll think it's the Lord.

I have been deceived so many times that I want to admonish you; do not respond immediately, unless you are sure you know who is speaking to you. A Sure way is to ask Jesus for help. Always the first thing to do is ask Jesus Who's speaking?

Something happened this morning and I'm allowed to share this with you. I have a routine every morning of greeting the Triune God individually, with a "Good Morning." I said the greeting, and waited, but I never got a response.

From experience I knew it was the Devil "blocking my communication." So I waited until I got in the den where I have spent my quiet time with the Lord, and I started saying the 15 scriptures that the Lord had instructed me to say every morning as my covering. When I finished, I heard inside of me, "I'll be back".

He leaves because he can't stand to hear the Word of God, or the Name of Jesus. So don't fear him. Keep the Switch of Faith turned on!

Fear Not, because Greater Is He that is in you than he that is in the world, 1st John 4:4; or use Psalm 91; it's full of protection.

Use the Word of God, the Power of the Name of Jesus, and by the Blood of the Lamb; we overcome. Revelation 12:11

Believe that you are already kept

Psalm 91
(A secret hiding place)

I personalize, You for me.

"He that dwells in the secret place of the most
High shall abide under the shadow of the Almighty.

I will say of the Lord, He is my refuge and my fortress; my God'
in Him will I trust.

Surely He shall deliver me from the snare of the fowler, and
from the noisome pestilence.

He shall cover me with His feathers, and under His wings shall
you trust: His truth shall be your shield and buckler,

I shall not be afraid for the terror by night; nor for the arrow
that flies by day:

Nor for the pestilence that walks in darkness; nor for the
destruction that wastes at noonday.

A thousand shall fall at my side, and ten thousand at my right
hand; but it shall not come near me."

"Only with my eyes shall I behold and see the reward of
the wicked.

"Because I have made the Lord, which is my refuge, even the
most High, my habitation:

There shall no evil befall me, neither shall any plague come
nigh my dwelling.

For He shall give His Angels charge over me; They shall bear
me up in their hands, lest I dash my foot against a stone.

I shall tread upon the lion and the adder: the young lion and the dragon shall I trample under feet.

Because I have set my Love upon Him. therefore will He deliver me: I will set him on high, because he has known my name.

He shall call upon Me, and I will answer him: I will be with him in trouble; I will deliver you, and honour you.

With long life will He satisfy me, and show me my salvation."

Just remember, God's Word is our defensive weapon and we can defeat Him every time. There's another way to respond when he attacks, just respond with the Words of Jesus, "He said "It is written! And he will leave. Remember Jesus used "It Is Written" in the wilderness, being tempted 40 days; so let's do what Jesus did; He's our example.

My favorite verse that I like to tell the Devil is, "Greater is He that is in me than he that is the world." God's Word never fails! He leaves. 1John4:4

Quote this one and he'll leave, "For I am persuaded, that neither death, nor life, nor Angels nor principalities, nor powers, nor things present, nor things to come; nor height, nor depth, nor any other creature, shall be able to separate us, me, from the love of God, which is in Christ Jesus our Lord." Romans 8:38

Chapter 15

What we Have in Christ

"In whom, Jesus, we have redemption through His Blood, even the forgiveness of our sins." Colossians 1:14

"Though our sins be red as scarlet, they shall be as white as snow." Isaiah 1:18

"We have freedom in Christ"
By the Blood of Jesus, we were "freed from the spiritual LAW of sin and death." Galatians 3:13

"We have healing in Christ"
"And by His stripes we are healed."
1st Peter 2:24

"We have Deliverance in Christ"
We were "delivered from the power of darkness and translated into the kingdom of His dear Son." Revelation 3:20 and 1st John 5:11-13

"We've been made new in our spirit."
"We are new creatures in Christ Jesus."
2 Corinthians 5:17

"We have life everlasting." John 3:16

"We are cleansed" when we read the Bible. John 15:3 and Ephesians 5:26

Nay, in all these things we are more than conquerors through Him, Jesus, that loved us. Romans 8:37

"We have Oneness in Christ"
We are "One in the Lord." Romans 8:2"
We are the righteousness of God by faith in Christ Jesus."
Psalm 91:4

Remember these words?

"I have whatever I say." Mark 11:23

"Lord, you are my refuge and strength."
Psalm 91:2

"In Him do I live and move and have my being." Acts 17:28a

"You will never leave me nor forsake me." Hebrews 13:5

"By His stripes I was healed, therefore, by His stripes I am healed by the Grace of God."
1Peter 2:24

"My God shall supply all my needs, according to His riches in Glory by Christ Jesus." Philippians 4:19

"Jesus is covering us with His feathers and under His wings we are trusting." Psalm 91:4

God's Promises

"But God is faithful, who will not allow you to be tempted above that you are able; but will with the temptation also make a way to escape, that you may be able to bear it."
1st Corinthians 10:13b

"All things work together for those who love God." Romans 8:28

"Surely goodness and mercy shall follow me all the days of my life." Psalm 23:6

"The Lord is my keeper. The Lord shall preserve me from all evil; He shall preserve my soul. He shall preserve my going out and coming in from this time forth and even for evermore." Psalm 121:7, 8

A reminder from the Lord:
"There is no need for you to fret about tomorrow, for the Father knows what you need, even before you ask Him. For I have you in the palm of my hand."

"Beloved, I wish above all things that you prosper and be in good health." 3rd John 2

"The thoughts that I have towards you are thoughts of peace and not of evil, and to give you an expected end." Jeremiah 29:11

"So shall My Word be that goes forth out of my mouth, shall not return unto Me void, but shall accomplish that which I please, and prosper in the way wherein I sent it." Isaiah 55:11

"Fear not, for I am with you: be not dismayed; for I am your God: I will strengthen you; yea, I will help you; yea, I will uphold you with the right hand of my righteousness." Isaiah 41:10

"Jesus said, I will never leave you nor forsake you." Hebrews 13:5

"They that wait on the Lord shall renew their strength; they shall mount up with wings as eagles; they shall run, and not be weary; and they shall walk and not faint." Isaiah 40:31

Chapter 16

Words to Use in Battle

" Greater is He that is in me than he that is in the world." 1st John 4:4

"No weapon formed against me shall prosper." Isaiah 54:17

"The gates of Hell shall not prevail against me." Matthew 16:18

"For God has not given me a spirit of fear, but of power, love and of a sound mind."
2nd Timothy 1:7

"I am seated with God in the heavens." Ephesians 2:6

"I will say of the Lord, He is my refuge and strength, a Very present help in trouble."
Psalm 91:2

"For God has in charge Angels over me, to keep me in all of my ways." Psalm 91:11

Be Doers of the Word

"I will present to God my body as a living sacrifice; Holy, and acceptable unto God, which is my reasonable service."
Romans 12:1

"I will seek first the kingdom of God and His righteousness, and all these other things will be added unto " Matthew 6:3

"I will love the Lord my God with all my heart, and with all my soul, and with all of my mind, and my neighbor as myself." Matthew 22:37,39

"I will "Enter His gates with thanksgiving and into His courts with Praise." Psalm 100:4

"I will renew my mind by the Word of God every day; and be not conformed to this world, but be transformed by the renewing of my mind." Romans 12:2

I will live by faith, to have the God kind of faith listed next: God called Abraham a father of many nations, when he was 90 some years old;

God said to Abram, "I have made you a father of many nations, Abraham, before him whom he believed, even God, who quickens the dead and calls those things that be not as though they were." Romans 4:17 (That's the God Kind of Faith)

"God calls those things that be not as though they were." Romans 4:17

And we are to do what the Word of God tells us to say and do, by faith.

That's confessing what you believe before you see it.

A man's belly shall be satisfied with the fruit of his mouth; and with the increase of his lips shall he be filled.

Death and life are in the power of the tongue; and they that love it shall eat the fruit thereof. Proverbs 18:20,21

What the Word is Like

"The Word of God is quick and powerful, sharper than any two edged sword." Hebrews 4:12

"So then, Faith comes by hearing and hearing by the Word of God." Romans 10:17

"The words that I speak unto you are Spirit and they are life." John 6:63b

"For they are life unto those that find them and health to all their flesh." Proverbs 4:22

"Thy Word have I hid in my heart that I might not sin against you. Psalm 119:11

"So shall My Word be, that goes forth out of My mouth: it shall not return unto Me void but it shall accomplish that which I please, and it shall prosper in the thing whereto I sent it." Isaiah 55:11

Chapter 17

Spiritual Laws

The Law of Love:

I for one fall short of this every day; but I remember one day however, I was aware I showed love to someone, when after the deed was done, I heard inside of me, "You just fulfilled the Law of Love."

That was a surprise to me because I never heard Love in that way, that Love is a LAW. I haven't even thought about it like that before, being a LAW, Have you?

Then my mind went to the first and second commandment; am I walking in Love? I just realized that it's actually a sin if we aren't, and out of the will of God for sure. When I feel the sense of guilt I quickly ask for forgiveness, according to 1ˢᵗ John 1:9.

Are we able to walk in Love all the time? No, I don't think so; as no one is perfect; and the Lord reminds me too that it is "All Grace." Thank you Lord God. (I heard inside, You're Welcome.)

Spiritual Laws are a sure thing to happen, just like the Law of Gravity.

•   The LAW of LOVE. Galatians 5:14, Romans 13:8

- There's the LAW of LIBERTY. James 1:25

- The LAW of the SPIRIT of LIFE in CHRIST JESUS. Romans 8:2

- The LAW of ONENESS. James 2:8; 2nd Corinthians 5:17

- The LAW of FAITH. Romans 3:27

- The LAW of SOWING and REAPING. Luke 6:38

- The LAW of Christ. Galatians 6:2

Apply the Law of Christ

1. Be willing to Listen who are different: like, "tell me more, what's your feeling."

2. Be willing to learn. Be students and not critics.

3. Be willing to Love. Christ died for us while we were ye sinners, Love Him and others back for what He did for us.

4. Refuse Labels. It's demeaning to the core of our identity; Christ died for them too.

5. "Put Allegiance To Christ first and His Kingdom; and loving people without animosity."

"Jesus built His church, which lasted centuries, and "the Gates of Hell" shall not prevail against them." Matthew 16:18
(The Roman Empire didn't last, it failed.)

"For the Law of the Spirit of Life in Christ Jesus has made us Free from the Law of Sin and Death" Romans 8:2

"Whosoever looks into the Perfect Law of Liberty and continues therein; he being not a forgetful hearer, but a doer of the Word." James 1:25

"Bear one another's burdens, and so fulfill the Law of Christ." I asked the Lord what does this mean? He said, "Support them." Galatians 6:2

The Law of Sowing and Reaping

"Be not deceived; God isn't mocked; for whatsoever a man sows that shall he also reap." Galatians 6:7

"Give and it shall be given unto you, good measure, press down and shaken together, shall men give unto your bosom. For with the same measure that you give, it shall be measured to you again." Luke 6:38

That's the Spiritual Law at work in our lives.

The Law of Faith

"God has set forth to be a propitiation through faith in His Blood, to declare His righteousness for the remission of sins that are past, through the forbearance of God; To declare, I say, at this time His righteousness; that He might be the justifier of him which believes in Jesus."

Where is the boasting then? It is excluded. By what Law? Of Works? No; but by the Law of Faith." Romans 3:27

"Without faith it is impossible to please God. for He that comes to God must believe that He is, and that He is a rewarder of them that diligently seek Him." Hebrews 11:6

The Law of Love

"For all the Law is fulfilled in one word, even in this; Thou shalt love thy neighbor as thyself." Galatians 5:14

The Law of Prosperity

"Beloved I wish above all things that you prosper and be in good health." 3rd John:2

I believe that it is God's will for us to prosper; therefore I have whatsoever I say; "I prosper and I am in good health." Mark 11:23

Chapter 18

Keeping the Door Closed to the Enemy

Door #1–Give no place to the Devil in Jesus' Name.
Door #2 – Control your thoughts and your body.
Door #3 – Submit yourself unto God and resist the Devil.
Door #4 –Ask forgiveness, and quickly forgive others.

Explanations:

Door #1 – Means to speak to your mountain.
Door #2 – Use the Keys to Heaven,

Bind and loose

Door #3 – Control Negative thoughts.
Door #4 – Submit to God, resist the Devil.
Door #5 –" Be ye Holy as I am Holy, says the Lord."

Our minds are the place that the Devil comes to test us; for he knows our weaknesses and is familiar with our ways, because he watches us. We have to deal with him on a daily basis until we die; So get used to it and learn to control Him. Not the other way around; so plead the Blood of Jesus over your mind, and even ask for Jesus' help if there is confusion.

Every believer has the TOOLS for life, found in the Word of God. So, We overcome In the Name of Jesus: First You Bind the strongman, Matthew 12:29, and in Jesus' Name, demand the spirit of, name the issue you have, and loose that spirit on earth as it is in heaven. Matthew 18:18

"It is done as I have said, In the Name of Jesus." Mark 11:23
We have the Victory over the enemy every time.
Revelation 12:11

The Word of God as it is written, "God has given us everything we need pertaining to life and godliness." 2nd Peter 1:3

"trust in the Lord with all of your heart and lean not unto your own understanding. In all your ways acknowledge Him, and He will direct your path. Proverbs 3:5

"My Word is a Lamp unto your feet and a Light unto your path"; and become a doer of the Word. For Jesus said, "My Words will never fail; they are from everlasting to everlasting."
Psalm 119:105

The Power of the Word

Here's an EXAMPLE:

One day a friend of mine called me and shared with me that "I believe my husband is going to kill me. What do you think I should do?" I said, You should use the Word; just say, "No weapon formed against me shall prosper."

It wasn't long after that she called back and said, "My husband cornered me and had his hands around my throat, and I said those words, "No weapon formed against me shall prosper." And he backed off! And He said, "I should have done it sooner."

To my surprise, a little later another person called me and said "that she was being abused verbally by her husband;" So I gave her the same scripture; and Later her response was exactly the same; "He backed off."

See how God works? Why two times in a row that specific Word was given and the results were the same.? Because God knew I would remember it and put it here. Doesn't God know all, from the end to the beginning?

This Promised Word of truth is found in Isaiah 54:17, and it works.

Chapter 19

Scriptures of Our Authority

I n Jesus Name, "I have the authority over ALL the power of the enemy and nothing by any means shall hurt me." Luke 10:19

God will always back up His Name and His Word. The Devil is afraid of that Name.

That at the Name of Jesus every knee should bow; of things in heaven, things in earth and things under the earth." Philippians 2:10

"In JESUS ' NAME I cast out devils." Mark 16:17,18

"In Jesus' Name, I overcome, by the Blood of the Lamb and the word of my testimony."
Revelations 12:11

"Jesus said, I will give unto you the keys of the Kingdom of heaven; and whatsoever you shall bind on earth shall be bound in heaven; and whatsoever you shall be loosed on earth shall be loosed in heaven." Matthew 16:19

My husband needed to take the drug Eliquis, it's a blood thinner; and we were in a cabin on our vacation, and upon waking in the morning, my husband's pillow was saturated with blood. They didn't tell us that would happen and was ignorant of the side-effects, but learned very quickly.

How nice it had stopped, but needed to wait a week to see our Doctor, which we did. Our Doctor said he needed to be on that drug. So I thought the best thing for me to do is to speak to Eliquis. Speak to your mountain; Mark 11:23

I said, "I plead the blood of Jesus over this pill; over Jim, David, our son, and me, Lord Jesus, I'm going to ask you to keep Jim's nose from bleeding day or night, or anywhere else on his body from the side effects of this pill. The Word says we can ask to receive, which we do and we thank you for it, in your precious Name, Jesus." Amen. Matthew 7:7

I have been saying this prayer every day since that first medication, and I Thank the Lord that his nose bled just once. Jesus always hears and answers when we call on Him; He is so faithful. A person should pray over all your meds because of the side effects.

Chapter 20

Faith

"So then, Faith comes by hearing, and hearing by the Word of God." Romans 10:17

"Faith works by Love." Galatians 5:6b

When you understand that we can claim the Word of God as a believer, we can say like Jesus said, "It is written," when He was confronted by the Devil in the wilderness. That's what Faith is all about. Trusting in what the Word of God says, and acting on that Word.

Galatians 5:1 Means standing in Faith of the Word and with confidence in what you have said to believe in your heart; that you have chosen this position, therefore you qualify to be protected from whatever or whenever the Devil attacks you.

Or use Psalm 91:1,2 In what you say, It is written:

"Because "I have made the Most High my habitation; No evil shall befall me, no plague shall come nigh my dwelling, because He has given His Angels charge over me to keep me in all my ways;" and that includes the attack of Covid Virus.

Just because some of you probably know more than I, doesn't mean you don't need to hear this again.

But this, I do know, that the Word of God is Spirit and it is life, and it is needed to be fed upon, like food is to our bodies. That's how our faith grows; by hearing and hearing what it says; and as years go by, that Word goes deep into our hearts or spirit, and we become rooted and grounded in the love of God by Christ Jesus.

It's a wonderful feeling to know a person can be one with God the Father, God the Son and empowered by His Holy Spirit, at the same time; because they are One, so are we with them. Being one with God is awesome! Which is God's perfect will.

Then we will not be ashamed when we see Him, at His coming.

Why should we doubt His Words? It is written: He is the Word.

Our need then is having our minds renewed in the spirit of the living Word of God." For the carnal mind is enmity against God. Just like Jesus said To Nicodemus, "You need to be born again." John 3:4-7

John tells us, "It is He, Jesus, who Baptizes with the Holy Ghost." (That's who the change comes from) John 1:35

"For unto us was the gospel preached, as well as unto them; but the Word preached did not profit them; Not being mixed with faith in them that heard it."
Without faith, it's impossible to please God." Hebrews 11:6

"Therefore being justified by faith, we have peace with God through our Lord Jesus Christ." Romans 5:1

What do you think is God's concern for you?

From all the years I have learned and heard, is what's foremost that God desires for you to be One with Him, so He can shower you with "His Grace and Peace, from God the Father, and from the Lord Jesus."

There are two verses that are given me often, they are; "The thoughts that I have toward you are thoughts of peace and not of evil, and to give you an expected end." Jeremiah 29:11

The other one is; "I wish above all things that you prosper and be in good health, even as your soul prospers." 3rd John 2

God has your best interest at heart, and is concerned about the things we are concerned about.

"A Word of Wisdom"

"Faithlessness will bring doubt as fast as anything."

Faithlessness would be a hindrance, along with Fear, doubt and unbelief. The Lord says about fear, "Don't do it"

Our attention must be on the Word and not on the circumstances. The Word brings hope, and Faith that sees it now! It is NOW FAITH that pleases God. I'm still learning that one.

"Then He, Jesus, said unto him, "Thomas, Reach here your finger, and behold My hands; and reach here your hand, and thrust it into My side; and be not faithless, but believing." John 20:27

Chapter 21

Living in the Covenant of His Blood

Pleading the Blood:

This phrase has become a fixed one for me, as I'm using it on a daily basis; because one day my husband and I were getting onto an airplane to go on a cruise, and just before we were to board, the Word of the Lord came to me and said, "When you put your first step on the plane, plead the Blood."

Think about it, that Jesus is claiming His own Blood has the power over the safety of that flight. So I did what He said, because I believed His Word and about His BLood.

This day surprised me as well, but maybe it shouldn't have. The Lord said to me one Sunday morning going into our church; He said, "When you put your first step into your church, Plead the Blood."

What do you think of that? Surely there are evil spirits around us all the time, even in our churches, because I have been deceived regarding water Baptism while sitting in the pew. Not only that, The Blood protects us from keeping the Devil off our minds, even from blocking our communications with God.

We no longer live under Satan's power or authority, when we belong to Jesus; for God translated us into the Kingdom of His Son. Luke 12:32

"It is the Father's good pleasure to give us the kingdom; He has told me. "

"We are DELIVERED from the power of darkness and translated into the Kingdom of light and Life." Colossians 1:13

WHAT WE HAVE and WHO WE ARE In Christ Jesus."

We have SALVATION: Which is, Deliverance, Healing, Preservation and wholeness; according to Vine's Dictionary.

"We are CRUCIFIED with Christ." Galatians 2:20

"We are BAPTIZED into Christ's death."
Galatians 3:27,28

"Jesus BAPTIZES us in the HOLY GHOST." Acts 2:4 He will, if you ask HIM.

We were "REDEEMED from the Curse of the Law" by the BLood of Jesus.

Galatians 3:13

The curses of the Law:

Are sickness and death; And they are listed in Deuteronomy 28:15 and below.

"The LAW of the Spirit of Life in Christ Jesus has made us FREE from the LAW of sin and death." Romans 8:2

And Jesus has "washed us from sins in His Blood." Revelation 1:5

We were RAISED UP TOGETHER to SIT TOGETHER with God in the heavens.
Ephesians 2:6

We shall REIGN in THIS LIFE, AS KINGS and PRIESTS. Romans 5:17; Revelation 1:6

I Believe the Truth of the Word of God. I believe we were created in the image of God. God is a Spirit, therefore we are spirit; we have a soul (which is our mind, will and emotions) and we live in a body. 1st Thessalonians 5:23

If you have received Jesus into your heart, or spirit, Your spirit is One with God's Spirit. God is everlasting, therefore, you too and will live forever with Him. Revelation 3:20

Question? Where then does our heart or spirit reside in our body? Certainly it isn't the heart that physically pumps blood, because it isn't a spirit, and it dies.

"He that believes on me, as the scripture has said, out of his belly shall flow rivers of living water; but this is He, Jesus, said of the Spirit, which they that believed on Him, Jesus, should receive." John 7:38,39

Chapter 22

"I Believe"

~~~

T hat Christ's spiritual life and love dwells in us, flowing out like a mighty river. I think that it's the same place where Mary received the Holy Spirit.

It was revealed to me "that the Spirit of Jesus resides in the center of our being;" and I have experienced Christ's presence in my belly that is warm and comforting. John 7:38 Hallelujah!

The Lord said to me, "That Psalm 91:1-4 is the secret place and that place was for me."

I quoted Him exactly, but God's Word is for every believer to act on the Written Words of God. His Words.

It is our secret hiding place; a place of refuge from the enemy; and it's good to say what one believes, like to say what this next Word tells us to do.

"Abide in Me and I in you; as the branch cannot bear fruit of itself, except it abides in the vine, no more can you except you abide in Me." John 15:4

This was revealed to me also, "That every time when you see the word "Cover," in the Word, it always means protection."

Jesus replied, "My feathers are always around you." "I am the vine and you are the branches; He that abides in Me, and I in him, the same brings for much fruit; for without Me you can do nothing." John 15:5

Let's look at the Scriptures that have been given us to claim healing.

"That it might be fulfilled which was spoken by the prophet Isaiah, saying, "Himself took our infirmities and bare our sickness." Matthew 8:17

"Who, Jesus, Himself bare our sins in His own body, on the tree, that we being dead to sins, should live unto righteousness; by whose stripes we were healed." 1st Peter 2:24

"But He, Jesus, was wounded for our transgressions, He was bruised for our iniquities, the chastisement of our peace was upon Him; and with His stripes we are healed." 40 lashes. Isaiah 53:5

Let's look at Mark 11:23,24. TWO things are necessary, speak it and receive it, before you see it. That's NOW FAITH; now you can claim that you have it.

Hindrances to Faith

We all have been given a measure of faith, and the one thing I do know about faith, is that if we don't have faith, "it's impossible to please God." Hebrews 11:6

For it is written, that "the just shall live by faith," Romans 1:17

In fact, there is a "Law of Faith, if we believe." Romans 3:27

Hindrances to our faith are:

- Our minds; reasoning over what the Word of God says.
- Our own wills: or the lusts of the flesh.
- Our emotions: or not focusing on the Word.
- Not being a doer of the Word.
- Lack of Obedience to the Word

Believing, but not mixed with faith; knowing that you have it when you pray and not after.

Believe the Word when it says, "For every one that asks receives." Luke 11:10

Lack of Receiving Christ

"Behold I stand at the door and knock; if any man hears My voice and opens the door, I will come into him and sup with him, and he with Me." Revelation 3:20

This is the Oneness Jesus talked about; so that our spirits would become filled with His Spirit. "Therefore, If any man be in Christ, he is a new creature: Old things are passed away; behold, ALL things become New." 2Corinthians 5:17

"And this is the record that God has given to us eternal life, and this life is in His Son;

"He that has the Son has life; and he that has not the Son has not life. 1st John 5:11-,12

God's Word Calls us "More than conquerors."

"No, in all things we are more than conquerors through Himthat loved us."
Romans 8:37

Why? "Because, "Jesus is the Greater One in us, than he that is in the world."

So We can use the power of the Word backed up by Jesus' Name, that He gave us to use."
1st John 4:4, Mark 16:17, Mark 11:23, Luke 10:19

This verse, "Greater is He that is in me than he that is in the world." I have repeated many times in the book for your sake; because we aren't being taught to confess the Word, that we have power.

"The Word loses its power when it isn't spoken, said Jesus." From experience I can tell you that the Word works.

One day I was watching Pat Robertson's show, and he was talking about his experience of a tornado coming from the sea, heading straight towards his building that's on the coast. This is what he said, speaking directly to the tornado,

"In the Name of Jesus," "I Command you to go back from whence you came. And the tornado took a sharp U turn and headed back into the sea."

Oh, I said, I can do that." So the next opportunity came that a tornado was reported heading toward our house and county; it was in a straight path towards my house, our daughters' and son's houses and right towards Mark and our daughter Charlene's house; So I went outside and spoke;
I said the first thing that came to my mind:

"In the Name of Jesus I speak to the Prince of the air. "I thought that was proper.

Then I said, ""You will not bring your destruction here at my house, or to the houses of my family; and I named them because they were right in a row heading East. (I remembered that I have whatsoever I say. Mark 11:23)

"So I said, "In the Name of Jesus, It is done."

The next day I heard from our son in law, tell about what happened last night; as their house was in line in the next state.

He said, "I was watching the radar pretty close, and he said, "I couldn't believe my eyes; but the tornado literally, you know, split and went around both sides of my house." He continued; "I couldn't believe what I saw, but it's true."

Since then, the Lord not only approved what I had said and done, He now tells me just when I should go out and what to say; and I don't use the Prince of the Air anymore.

Now I go outside and just start out with;

"In the Name of Jesus You are not allowed to bring your destruction here, nor any of my household houses; then I name their cities. Then I say It is done, In the Name of Jesus."

Also, by the Grace of God I can share this:
For God has said, "I have called you to be a witness of the power of God." It's God's power not only for me, but the Word of God says that it's for ALL Believers to use the Name of Jesus; Over all the power of the enemy and nothing by any means shall hurt you." Luke 10:19; and Mark 16:17.

Chapter 23

Jesus' Victory

Jesus' Victory on the cross was not the only place He demonstrated His power; because when He showed up in Hell to face the Devil;

The Devil was pleased he got Jsus killed, but I'm sure it gave the Devil goose bumps when He saw Him show up in Hell and not in the grave.

All hell broke loose and the war began; as it is written, "And having spoiled principalities and powers, He made a show of them openly." Jesus paraded the Devil before his demons, and made a show of Him, triumphing over him in it, and took the keys of death and hell from him. Colossians 2:15, Revelation 1:18

"Then God raised us up together to sit together in Christ, in the heavens; What joy filled my heart to learn this is my position in Christ." To Reign in this life by One Jesus Christ." That's our position of authority.

Ephesians 2:6; "Reigning in this life by One Lord Jesus Christ." (Because we are one with Him on the Cross, in death and in the resurrection)

This was revealed to me that "It is the Fathers' good pleasure to give you the Keys to the." kingdom." Matthew 16:19

Whatever you bind on earth is bound in heaven; whatever is loosed on earth is loosed in heaven." (But first bind the strongman) Matthew 16:19

That gave me guts to go after everything bad that I inherited.

"The Lord wants you to know that there is power in this Word:" "You have whatsoever we say." Mark 11:23

The word "say" is mentioned three times in this one verse, so it's telling you to pay attention to what it's telling us what we can do and say.

It tells you to do and start Confessing that, because you said yes to Jesus, You have Him inside. "For greater is He that is in You than he that is" in the world." 1st John 4:4

We are more than Conquerors, in JesusName. Romans 8:37

During the time I was with Women's Aglow women, as I mentioned at the beginning of the book, my life changed when I received the Baptism of the Holy Spirit during that time.

I grew spiritually; and over a period of time the Holy Spirit gave me a gift of "the Word of Wisdom;"and Also, the Word of Knowledge.

it was from the promptings of the Holy Spirit, that it was God's will for me to write this book, and to show forth the power of God and His Word.

I'm still open to learn more of what the Word of God says of my rights and privileges. this is the time to show you just what I mean.

Here's an illustration of God's power, when "Peter came to the gate Beautiful; and saw a lame man.

He said to the lame man, "Silver and gold have I none; but such as I have, give I thee: In the name of Jesus Christ of Nazareth rise up and walk." "He stood up and walked into the temple, praising God." Acts 3:6

Did you notice that he didn't pray for him? He just spoke the Truth of God's Word, just like what we can say and do; just like us Christans should do also.

This is new to me, that we can command the Devil in Jesus Name; we have the right and privilege over the Devil. "The Lord said that he is obligated to do it."

Compare these two verses: "And whatsoever you shall ask anything in My Name, that will I do that the Father may be Glorified in the Son." John 14:13-14

"And in that day you shall ask me nothing. Verily, verily, I say unto you, Whatsoever you shall ask the Father in My Name, He will give it to you. Hitherto have you asked nothing in my Name; as, and you shall receive, that your joy may be full." John 16:23,24

The difference between these 2 verses is: that the Father is mentioned here in connection with prayer, but He is not mentioned in the Word of God in John chapter 14.

So I understood then that I could demand, by the grace of God and in the Name of Jesus, "to bind first the strongman on earth as it is in heaven; and then in Jesus' Name, I bind the spirit of osteoporosis on earth as it is in heaven. Then I demanded in the Name of Jesus you Strongman, I loose the osteoporosis off my body, on earth as it is in heaven. It is done as I have said. "

Jesus said, "but first bind the strongman is in Matthew 12:29; and loose on earth as it is in heaven." Matthew 18:18

As It is written, "I have whatsoever I say." Mark 11:23 "You glorified Me as well as the Father". Thank you for that, I responded.

These verses are how we, the church, should deal with the Devil.

"The gates of Hell shall not prevail against me." Matthew 16:18

I choose the Law of Faith: I will not fear; I resist the Devil in the Name of Jesus.

I am peaceful, and I will be still under all circumstances, for God is with and for me.

It is written – "No weapon formed against me shall prosper." Isaiah 54:17

It is written – "Greater is He that is in me than he that is in the world."1John 4:4

"Jesus has set me free," and I am free indeed.
Romans 8:2

It is written – "I can do all things through Christ who strengthens me." Philippians 4:13

"God will help me, strengthen me and uphold me with His righteous right hand." Isaiah 41:10

"He shall cover you with His feathers. And;
"There shall no evil befall me, neither shall any plague come nigh
my dwelling, for He shall give His angels charge over me to keep
me in all of my ways." Psalm 91:4, 9 10

"I stand fast in the liberty wherewith Christ has made us free."
Galatians 5:1

It is written – "By His stripes I was healed," so by His stripes I
am healed;" by the Grace of God. 1st Peter 2:24

It is written – "I will never leave you nor forsake you." Hebrews 13:5

I will say of the Lord, You are my refuge and my fortress." And
"I have whatsoever I say." Mark 11:23

"The Lord shall preserve my going out and coming in, now and
forever." Psalm 121:8

"There shall no evil befall me, no plague come nigh my dwelling,
for He has given His Angels charge over you to keep you in all
of your ways." Psalm 91:10,11

"I will say of the Lord, He is my refuge and my fortress; my God;
in Him will I trust." Psalm 91:2

"He shall cover me with His feathers, and under His wings I shall
trus; His truth is my shield and my buckler," Psalm 91:4

Faith In Action

"I Stand fast therefore in liberty; and be not entangled again with
the yoke of bondage."
Galatians 5:1

Reigning in Life Because of Jesus' victory over Satan at the Cross, we can reign as Kings in this life here in this world; . Because we are in Christ, Satan is under Jesus' feet. Jesus is our head, we are His body and the enemy is under His feet. We don't have to struggle to be victorious; we just need to stand our ground using God's Word against a defeated foe. Here is how to do that.

Romans 5:17

Pleading the blood of Jesus against the Devil is our victory over him; because of the shed blood of Jesus. When we plead the blood against the Devil, we are really pleading our covenant rights of protection against the enemy.

Isaiah 54:17; Luke 10:19; Philippians 2:9,10; Colossians 1:13

Chapter 24

A Time to Reflect

N ow that I'm 83 years old, I wish to reflect back to the time when my family was young. Moving to another town was a busy time. Two of our four children were in grade school, and the last two 13 months apart.

I felt I could handle it all; which I did for a while; until they were in High school, and by then I got involved in **other activities**; until symptoms of a very loud buzzing in my ears showed up was too much to handle.

The noise I recall was like a florescent bulb; so I decided to see a Doctor.

I'll never forget the Doctor's first words, "**So what are you doing**?"

So I mentioned I was in the Choir at Church, I was President of the Women's group at church, I'm in a Bible study during the week, and just finished hanging curtains in the Sunday school room. I have four children that I drive one of the girls to dance lessons and pick up another after swimming lessons. Needless to say, it was a long list; and his advice was,
"**Go home and rest**."

Well, I surmised I had a burn out; but I also knew who would heal me; so I chose to rest at 2:00 every day and I found out that if I rested two hours, then the buzzing sound would leave.

It still amazes me as to how long it took for it to go away, was 15 years.

You also learn to prioritize!

The Word of Wisdom "Stillness is Wellness"

This was another reminder of the Goodness God gave to me a long time ago; how timely. It's just what I needed now.

The first words I ever heard from God was, "Be still and know that I am God."

It's been years before that was settled in my thinking. And over the years He has been working with me on being still and in peace; then God added saying, "Stillness is Wellness."

Have you learned how important being in peace means to our bodies?

Each day, sometimes twice in a day I would hear, "The Grace and Peace from God our Father and from the Lord Jesus Christ." Just a reminder to be at peace, no matter what's going on.

"Another one I would hear often is from the Holy Spirit of Jesus saying, "I see Grace flowing from the throne room of God." Oh, we have a God that lavishly loves us. He was blessing me; and His Grace of Love just flowed..

What I understand about this word of Grace He poured out; He's telling me that His Grace is sufficient for whatever I have to do that day.

God wants us always to be in Peace, because the result is good health; and it's bad health to FRET.

It's God's Grace, that He just poured out upon me; Flowing from the Throne Room of God, for my every need. WOW!

What a wonderful God we have, who cares for us and each person in the world at the same time. He just watches us so deeply, and with a watchful eye; knows just what we need and when.

Later in life, I've learned to love this verse, "Beloved, I wish above all things that you prosper and be in good health."

And if you listen to the Holy Spirit's leading, He can help you do that, for it is the will of God for every believer to be not only healthy but whole.

Since I have been blessed with the Spiritual gift of "the Word of Wisdom;" about Stillness is Wellness," was given to me as a guide to practice as well.

Then one day God chose to show me how to receive and to go about doing this Word of Wisdom of stillness: as there was a time in the day when I needed to give myself a shot for Osteoporosis.

God said: "On your lunch hour; cherish the time because This time is just for you." "Eat, of course; then find a place to be alone, where you can close your eyes and let go of all your thoughts. Quit worrying; don't be anxious; pray if you think you should, but then, let all your thoughts go and just rest."

To use a familiar phrase, "It's a time for charging one's battery." See howGod cares for you.?

Eat well, rest and "Take time just for You;" and Sleep well'. These are good steps to follow I think towards being well. Don't you agree?

Chapter 25

Reigning in life

B ecause of Jesus' victory over Satan at the Cross, we are seated with Christ and can reign as Kings in this life; here in this world now, because we are in Christ.

Satan is under our feet; for Jesus is our head and we are his body. Our feet are Jesus' feet. We don't have to struggle to be victorious; we just need to stand our ground using God's Word against a defeated foe. Ephesians 6:2, Romans 5:17

Here is how to do that;
Plead the Blood of Jesus over yourself for protection against the Devil; "In the Name of Jesus, I rebuke you Devil, for I have overcome you; because Greater is He that is in me, than he that is in the world." 1stJohn 4:4

He'll run because of the Blood and he's afraid of the Name of Jesus. Use this word against him that I use often, "No weapon formed against me shall prosper." Isaiah 54:17

Jesus used this word to Peter; "Upon this rock I will build my church; You say, "the gates of hell shall not prevail against me, for I am the church." We can do this, because God gave it to the Church and Jesus gave us the keys to heaven."

It is written in Matthew 16:18,19. It works!

Claim your Rights as an Overcomer

Our victory over Satan is because of the shed Blood of Jesus; and when we plead the Blood against the Devil, we are really pleading our covenant rights of protection against the enemy.

The Blood of Jesus that was shed on the cross, has delivered us from darkness and translated us into the Kingdom of His Son".

"Isaiah 54:17; 2nd Timothy 1:7, Philippians 2:9,10; Colossians 1:13

Stand on this: "And they overcame him by the blood of the Lamb, and by the word of their testimony." Revelation 12:11

YOU, "Resist the Devil in the Name of Jesus and he shall flee from you." He will. James 4:7

What makes him flee? Because he is afraid of the Name; and because "Greater is He that is in you than He that is in the world." 1st John 4:4

Use this one too, "No weapon formed against you shall prosper." Isaiah 54:17

We Overcome Because it is written in 1John4:4; and Revelation 12:11.

Angels

One day I called on the Lord, and He didn't answer. I did it again and called on Him, but He didn't answer. Then I got the picture.

I learned this from the Lord before, "That the Devil can block our communication with his presence." Then I started thinking; I'm going to call on my Guardian Angel; so I said to Him, "Guardian Angel, get the Devil out of here;" and He said, "No problem." Then I heard the Devil say, "OH! OH"! Psalm 91:1-11

Maybe I better ask the Lord, "Is it okay that I called on my Angel? " He answered, "You can use Him as many times as you like and wherever you like." **Hallelujah!**

You know what else I learned about my Angel? He's very Tall and BIG!!

What a help he has been to me since; and I might add quickly so is the Lord and the Holy Spirit we also can call upon. So why are we even a little bit fearful, when we can get help like that!

Also, we have as an heir of Salvation, Ministering Angels according to the Word Of God; for the purpose of helping us to get the money we need because our Heavenly Father doesn't have it in heaven to give.

Here is a common need we all have is money. Next I want to share with you what I have learned about acquiring money.

So when I found that out, every time I charged something, I asked my Ministering Angel to replace that exact amount; and when the first time I asked my Ministering Angel responded, "I'm on my way;" and I have continued doing so since. Hebrews 1:13,14

Thank you for covering me with your Angels for help and safety. Psalm 91 :11

Chapter 26

Precious Promises

"For God so loved the World that He gave His only begotten Son, that whosoever believes in Him, shall not perish but have everlasting life. John 3:16

"And we know that all things work together for good to them that love God; to them who are called according to His purpose." Romans 8:28

"Beloved, I wish above all things that you may prosper and be in good health, even as your soul prospers." 3rd John:2

One day the Lord asked, "where does it say in the Word, "I will never leave you nor forsake you? I said right away, "I don't know."

So I looked it up and found it in Hebrews 13:5b. It says, "I will never leave you nor forsake you," just like He said." Amen To That!

"Therefore I say unto you, what things soever you desire, when you pray, believe that you receive them and you shall have them." Mark 11:24

"Fear thou not; for I am with you: be not dismayed; for I am thy God. I will strengthen you; yea, I will help you; yea, I will uphold you with the right hand of My righteousness." Isaiah 41:10

This one is foremost in our Lord's thinking: "I wish above all things, that you prosper and be in good health. 3rd John2

Are you getting a picture here; how God is for us, and interested in every part of your body and life? It's just awesome to me to learn just how much He cares for us, Not only that, but He wants you to never fear; and His Word tells us that too. "For God didn't give us a spirit of fear, but of power, love. and of a sound mind."
2nd Timothy 1:7 God is for us!

Love is also top priority on a daily basis; and that He says; that it's just as important towards others, as it is to God. He puts Love at the very top, where it's needed.; Especially to one's husband; now at my older age,

I'm still learning something new from the heart of God; Don't let guilt take over, it's been dealt with through Jesus' death on the cross. "If we confess our sins He is faithful and just to forgive us our sins, and to cleanse us from all unrighteousness." 1stJohn 1:9

Chapter 27

Praise

Praise gets us into God's presence.

Praise is due a Holy God! Praising Him for who He is, and Praising God who is the Highest God: The one and only true God! The creator and sustainer of life.

It is by the Name of Jesus and by Blood of the Lamb, and by the Grace of God that we can come boldly into His presence. Hebrews 4:16

"Entering His gates with thanksgiving and entering His courts with PRAISE: be thankful and bless His Name." Psalm 100:4

Don't you think that after one blesses God that God won't bless you in return? He's just waiting for any opportunity to Bless His children.

That's His business of pouring out blessings each and every day. So don't forget to thank God for the little things in life. He gave it to us to enjoy.

"For the Lord God is a sun and shield; the Lord will give grace and glory; no good thing will He withhold from them that walk uprightly." Psalm 84:11

Genuine Praise is from the heart and not just from the head; the same is true when you read the Word of God. Are you doing it out of duty or love and reverence for God? It's called a sacrifice of Praise. Psalm 116:18

Praise: "I Will build your faith up and it will give you confidence so that you can say without any doubt, "God is on my side, I will not fear what man can do unto me."
Psalm 118:6

When the Word of God gets down in your spirit: and your mouth is filled with true praise from your heart; Sadness will turn into gladness, defeat turns to victory and your weakness goes from strength to strength, and your trials into triumph!

Consider this: Jesus has already defeated the enemy at the cross of Calvary. The victory has already been won for you, so in every circumstance you will ever face, you are covered through the covenant promises of God's Word; and the indwelling of God's faithful presence. 1st John 4:4

*Jesus said, "I a*m Alpha and Omega; the beginning and the ending says the Lord, which is, and which was, and which is to come, the Almighty." Revelation 1:8

Be Still and Enter Into His Rest

1. The rest for Christians is obtained by Faith.

"Let us therefore fear, lest a promise being left us of entering into His rest, any of you should seem to come short of it."

2. "For unto us was the gospel preached, as well as unto them: but the Word preached did not profit them, not being mixed with faith in them that heard it."

3. "For we which have believed do enter into rest, as HE said, as I have sworn in My wrath, if they shall enter into My rest: although the works were finished from the foundation of the world."

4. "For He said in a certain place of the seventh day this:; And God did rest the seventh day from all His works."

5. "And in this place again, if they shall enter into My rest."

6. "Seeing therefore it remains that some must enter therein, and they to whom it was first preached entered not in because of unbelief:

7. "Again He limits a certain day saying to David, today, after a long time; as it is said, today if you will hear His voice, harden not your hearts."

8. "For if Jesus had given them rest; then would He not afterward have spoken of another day."

9. "There remains therefore a rest to the people of God." Hebrews 13:5

God will not fail you; neither will His love diminish nor fade away; for Grace is in the Union, being one with Christ. God's Grace is the power and authority we have in Christ Jesus; and the way to win is having the confidence in the Name of Jesus.

"These signs shall follow them that believe; in My Name shall they cast out devils, they shall lay hands on the sick and they shall recover." Mark 16:17

"In Him Christ dwells all the fullness of the Godhead bodily. And you are complete in Him, Jesus, which is the head of all principality and power." Colossians 2:9,10

"At the Name of Jesus, every knee shall bow and every tongue confess, that Jesus Christ is Lord, to the Glory of God the Father." Philippians 2:10:11

No one can confess Jesus as Lord except by the Holy Ghost.

The Wells of our Salvation

"Jesus said to a crowd of people on the last day of the Feast; cried out and said, "If any man thirst let him come unto Me and drink. He that believes on Me as the scripture has said, out of his belly shall flow rivers of living water. But this He, Jesus, spoke of the Spirit, which they that believe in Him, Jesus, should receive." John 7:37

At one of the conferences I had attended, I remember we were lying on the floor in the presence of the Lord, and the Leader suggested, "Take a breath and drink in the Holy Spirit." As I was laying there, I was contemplating that if we didn't come and drink from our well of Salvation, would we become dry?

Surely, doing this we'd be honoring the presence of the Holy Spirit, for He is a person of the Trinity. Immediately, I heard inside, "Indeed, it is all what you have said it to be."

Chapter 28

"My Testimony"

⁓

I n 1974 after reading Isaiah 61, I heard inside of me, "This is for you."

It was after many years that this started to take place. I joined Women's Aglow International in 1982, a small group got together to pray, if you were interested in going into the prison, for the first time.

As I listened to each person volunteering, they all fit into the positions needed to fill; such as a speaker, the music, even to plan meals for their supper.

It all just fell into place, and all we needed now was an answer to our prayers to go in on a monthly basis; which happened. It was an old building, not big, but they had an oven to use to keep the food warm, as we each brought in something for dinner.

I knew right away that this was the door that I should walk through according to the first verse of Isaiah 61. We started out with 10 volunteers.

Soon they tore the old small building down and built a bigger and a newer facility with TV. After several years problems arose among the women, so there was more security, so only three volunteers were allowed to go in, and that included the speaker.

So I could see, after years being in there, some have left but also returned. Some of them are there for years.

I helped pray one on one with them, but I was privileged also to become a speaker. I recognized they would need steady help for getting into the Word, and to know where the verses are found. So I have supplied Bible Verses for them to read, three times a day. I made it up like a calendar for four years, as I saw they had nothing but time on their hands. Here is a sample. Maybe you would like to read the verses I chose too.

January 2009   (Morning, Noon and Night)

Sunday	Monday	Tuesday	Wednesday	Thursday	Friday	Saturday
				1 1John 1:9 1John 4:17 1Peter 1:4	2 Rmns 8:31 1John 3:8 Phil 4:19	3 2Tim 1:12 Col 2:15 James 4:8
4 Rmns 8:2 Rmns 8:35 Heb 10:23	5 2Cor 5:17 Matt 18,19 Eph 5:30	6 James 1:12 Heb 4:12 Eph 1:7	7 Heb 1:3 1John 4:17 Mark 9:23	8 Rmns8:32 1John 3:8b Gal 2:20	9 1John 4:4 Col 2:15 Ps 91	10 Col 3:9,10 Rmns 8:37 Eph 3:17
11 Col 1:27 Josh 1:9 Rmns 8:31	12 Col 3:4 Jere 33:3 Heb 13:8	13 1Cor 1:30 John 15:7 Isa 54:17	14 2Cor 13:5 John 16:24 Philp 4:13	15 Heb 13:5,6 Philp 4:19 Eph 3:20	16 John 1:12 1Pet 2:24 Ps 118:24	17 Isa 41:10 Ps 107:20 Ps 63:1-11
18 Matt 18:19 Eph 11:17 Ps 18:30	19 Mala 3:6 Gal 5:1 Ps 119:11	20 Ps 103 2Cor 10:4,5 Ps 119:50	21 Isa 53:5 Rmns 12:2 James 1:21	22 Jams 5:15,15 1John 5:4,5 Rmns 10:17	23 Prv 11:20,21 1John 5:12,13 Rmns 10:10	24 2Cor 12:10 3John 2 1Cor 13:13
25 Heb 11:6 Rmns 8:37 Ezek 12:25	26 Rmns 12:3 Prv 18:21 Dan 9:12	27 Rev 12:11 James 1:22 Matt 24:35	28 James 4:7 Josh 1:8 Rmns 4:21	29 Rmns 8:1,2 James 1:12 Rmns 10:9_	30 Rmns 12:1 Isa61:10 Acts 17:28	31 Isa 44:3 Isa41:10 Isa59:1

February 2009 — (Morning, Noon and Night)

Sunday	Monday	Tuesday	Wednesday	Thursday	Friday	Saturday
1 Ps 91:11 1Pet 2:24 1Peter 1:4	2 1John 4:4 Mark 11:23 Phil 4:19	3 Prv 4:20-22 Jam 4:7 Isa 41:10	4 Heb 13:5 Ps 103:1-6 Ps 91:2	5 John 6:63 1John 4:17 Gal 3:13	6 Rmns 8:31 1John 3:8 Ps 91	7 2Tim 1:12 Col 2:15 Isa 53:4,5
8 Rmns 8:2 Rmns 8:35 Heb 10:23	9 2Cor 5:17 Matt 18,19 Eph 5:30	10 James 1:12 Heb 4:12 Eph 1:7	11 Heb 1:3 1John 4:17 Mark 9:23	12 Rmns8:32 1John 3:8b Gal 2:20	13 1John 4:4 Col 2:15 Ps 91	14 Col 3:9,10 Rmns 8:37 Eph 3:17
15 Col 1:27 Josh 1:9 Rmns 8:31	16 Col 3:4 Jere 33:3 Heb 13:8	17 1Cor 1:30 John 15:7 Isa 54:17	18 2Cor 13:5 John 16:24 Philp 4:13	19 Heb 13:5,6 Philp 4:19 Eph 3:20	10 John 1:12 1Pet 2:24 Ps 118:24	21 Isa 41:10 Ps 107:20 Ps 63:1-11
22 Matt 18:19 Eph 11:17 Ps 18:30	23 Mala 3:6 Gal 5:1 Ps 119:11	24 Ps 103 2Cor 10:4,5 Ps 119:50	25 Isa 53:5 Rmns 12:2 James 1:21	26 Jams 5:15,15 1John 5:4,5 Rmns 10:17	27 Prv 11:20,21 1John 5:12,13 Rmns 10:10	28 2Cor 12:10 3John 2 1Cor 13:13

March 2009 — (Morning, Noon and Night)

Sunday	Monday	Tuesday	Wednesday	Thursday	Friday	Saturday
1 Rmns 8:2 Matt 8:17 Matt 16:18	2 3John :2 Ps 119:89,90 Phil 4:19	3 2Thess 3:3 Isa 40:31 Prv 23:7	4 Mrk 11:23 2Cor 6:16 1John 4:17	5 John 6:63 1John 4:17 1John 3:8	6 Rmns 8:31 1John 3:8 Col 2:15	7 2Tim 1:12 Col 2:15 Prv 3:5,6
8 Rmns 8:2 Rmns 8:35 Heb 10:23	9 2Cor 5:17 Matt 18,19 Eph 5:30	10 James 1:12 Heb 4:12 Eph 1:7	11 Heb 1:3 1John 4:17 Mark 9:23	12 Rmns8:32 1John 3:8b Gal 2:20	13 1John 4:4 Col 2:15 Ps 91	14 Col 3:9,10 Rmns 8:37 Eph 3:17
15 Col 1:27 Josh 1:9 Rmns 8:31	16 Col 3:4 Jere 33:3 Heb 13:8	17 1Cor 1:30 John 15:7 Isa 54:17	18 2Cor 13:5 John 16:24 Philp 4:13	19 Heb 13:5,6 Philp 4:19 Eph 3:20	20 John 1:12 1Pet 2:24 Ps 118:24	21 Isa 41:10 Ps 107:20 Ps 63:1-11
22 Matt 18:19 Eph 11:17 Ps 18:30	23 Mala 3:6 Gal 5:1 Ps 119:11	24 Ps 103 2Cor 10:4,5 Ps 119:50	25 Isa 53:5 Rmns 12:2 James 1:21	26 Jams 5:15,15 1John 5:4,5 Rmns 10:17	27 Prv 11:20,21 1John 5:12,13 Rmns 10:10	28 2Cor 12:10 3John 2 1Cor 13:13
29 Heb 11:6 Rmns 8:37 Ezek 12:25	30 Rmns 12:3 Prv 18:21 Dan 9:12	31 Rev 12:11 James 1:22 Matt 24:35				

April 2009 (Morning Noon and Night)

Sunday	Monday	Tuesday	Wednesday	Thursday	Friday	Saturday
			1 2Cor 6:16 1Pet 5:7 Matt 24:35	**2** Rmns 1:12 Col 2:11 1John 3:8	**3** Ps 16:11 Ps 34:7 Col 2:15	**4** Col 2:10,11 Ps 34:19 Rmns 3:23
5 Rmns 8:2 Rmns 8:35 Heb 10:23	**6** 2Cor 5:17 Matt 18,19 Eph 5:30	**7** James 1:12 Heb 4:12 Eph 1:7	**8** Heb 1:3 1John 4:17 Mark 9:23	**9** Rmns8:32 1John 3:8b Gal 2:20	**10** 1John 4:4 Col 2:15 Ps 91	**11** Col 3:9,10 Rmns 8:37 Eph 3:17
12 Col 1:27 Josh 1:9 Rmns 8:31	**13** Col 3:4 Jere 33:3 Heb 13:8	**14** 1Cor 1:30 John 15:7 Isa 54:17	**15** 2Cor 13:5 John 16:24 Philp 4:13	**16** Heb 13:5,6 Philp 4:19 Eph 3:20	**17** John 1:12 1Pet 2:24 Ps 118:24	**18** Isa 41:10 Ps 107:20 Ps 63:1-11
19 Matt 18:19 Eph 11:17 Ps 18:30	**20** Mala 3:6 Gal 5:1 Ps 119:11	**21** Ps 103 2Cor 10:4,5 Ps 119:50	**22** Isa 53:5 Rmns 12:2 James 1:21	**23** Jams 5:15,15 1John 5:4,5 Rmns 10:17	**24** Prv 11:20,21 1John 5:12,13 Rmns 10:10	**25** 2Cor 12:10 3John 2 1Cor 13:13
26 Heb 11:6 Rmns 8:37 Ezek 12:25	**27** Rmns 12:3 Prv 18:21 Dan 9:12	**28** Rev 12:11 James 1:22 Matt 24:35	**29** James 4:7 Josh 1:8 Rmns 4:21	**30** Rmns 8:1,2 James 1:12 Rmns 10:9_		

May 2009 (Morning, Noon and Night)

Sunday	Monday	Tuesday	Wednesday	Thursday	Friday	Saturday
					1 Rmns 8:31 1John 3:8 Phil 4:19	**2** 2Tim 1:12 Col 2:15 James 4:8
3 Rmns 8:2 Rmns 8:35 Heb 10:23	**4** 2Cor 5:17 Matt 18,19 Eph 5:30	**5** James 1:12 Heb 4:12 Eph 1:7	**6** Heb 1:3 1John 4:17 Mark 9:23	**7** Rmns8:32 1John 3:8b Gal 2:20	**8** 1John 4:4 Col 2:15 Ps 91	**9** Col 3:9,10 Rmns 8:37 Eph 3:17
10 Col 1:27 Josh 1:9 Rmns 8:31	**11** Col 3:4 Jere 33:3 Heb 13:8	**12** 1Cor 1:30 John 15:7 Isa 54:17	**13** 2Cor 13:5 John 16:24 Philp 4:13	**14** Heb 13:5,6 Philp 4:19 Eph 3:20	**15** John 1:12 1Pet 2:24 Ps 118:24	**16** Isa 41:10 Ps 107:20 Ps 63:1-11
17 Matt 18:19 Eph 11:17 Ps 18:30	**18** Mala 3:6 Gal 5:1 Ps 119:11	**19** Ps 103 2Cor 10:4,5 Ps 119:50	**20** Isa 53:5 Rmns 12:2 James 1:21	**21** Jams 5:15,15 1John 5:4,5 Rmns 10:17	**22** Prv 11:20,21 1John 5:12,13 Rmns 10:10	**23** 2Cor 12:10 3John 2 1Cor 13:13
24 Heb 11:6 Rmns 8:37 Ezek 12:25	**25** Rmns 12:3 Prv 18:21 Dan 9:12	**26** Rev 12:11 James 1:22 Matt 24:35	**27** James 4:7 Josh 1:8 Rmns 4:21	**28** Rmns 8:1,2 James 1:12 Rmns 10:9_	**29** Rmns 12:1 Isa61:10 Acts 17:28	**30** Isa 44:3 Isa41:10 Isa59:1

June 2009   (Morning, Noon and Night)

Sunday	Monday	Tuesday	Wednesday	Thursday	Friday	Saturday
	1 James 4:7 Rmns 8:1,2 John 6:63	2 Rmns 4:21 Rmns 8:31 1John 4:17	3 2Tim 1:12 1John 3:8 1Pet 1:4	4 1Pet 1:25 Matt 12:12 Lam 3:22,23	5 Heb 6:18 John 15:12 John 15:3-8	6 Ps 121:4-8 Matt 10:30 John 10:10
7 Rmns 8:2 Rmns 8:35 Heb 10:23	8 2Cor 5:17 Matt 18,19 Eph 5:30	9 James 1:12 Heb 4:12 Eph 1:7	10 Heb 1:3 1John 4:17 Mark 9:23	11 Rmns8:32 1John 3:8b Gal 2:20	12 1John 4:4 Col 2:15 Ps 91	13 Col 3:9,10 Rmns 8:37 Eph 3:17
14 Col 1:27 Josh 1:9 Rmns 8:31	15 Col 3:4 Jere 33:3 Heb 13:8	16 1Cor 1:30 John 15:7 Isa 54:17	17 2Cor 13:5 John 16:24 Philp 4:13	18 Heb 13:5,6 Philp 4:19 Eph 3:20	19 John 1:12 1Pet 2:24 Ps 118:24	20 Isa 41:10 Ps 107:20 Ps 63:1-11
21 Matt 18:19 Eph 11:17 Ps 18:30	22 Mala 3:6 Gal 5:1 Ps 119:11	23 Ps 103 2Cor 10:4,5 Ps 119:50	24 Isa 53:5 Rmns 12:2 James 1:21	25 Jams 5:15,15 1John 5:4,5 Rmns 10:17	26 Prv 11:20,21 1John 5:12,13 Rmns 10:10	27 2Cor 12:10 3John 2 1Cor 13:13
28 Heb 11:6 Rmns 8:37 Ezek 12:25	29 Rmns 12:3 Prv 18:21 Dan 9:12	30 Rev 12:11 James 1:22 Matt 24:35				

July 2009   (Morning, Noon and Night)

Sunday	Monday	Tuesday	Wednesday	Thursday	Friday	Saturday
			1 John 15:3 John 15:5 John 7,8	2 Jere 31:3 Matt 12:12 Ps 89:33,34	3 Ps 92:121 Ps 1:23 Gal 5:1	4 Eph 6:6 Eph 4:6,7 John 1:1
5 Rmns 8:2 Rmns 8:35 Heb 10:23	6 2Cor 5:17 Matt 18,19 Eph 5:30	7 James 1:12 Heb 4:12 Eph 1:7	8 Heb 1:3 1John 4:17 Mark 9:23	9 Rmns8:32 1John 3:8b Gal 2:20	10 1John 4:4 Col 2:15 Ps 91	11 Col 3:9,10 Rmns 8:37 Eph 3:17
12 Col 1:27 Josh 1:9 Rmns 8:31	13 Col 3:4 Jere 33:3 Heb 13:8	14 1Cor 1:30 John 15:7 Isa 54:17	15 2Cor 13:5 John 16:24 Philp 4:13	16 Heb 13:5,6 Philp 4:19 Eph 3:20	17 John 1:12 1Pet 2:24 Ps 118:24	18 Isa 41:10 Ps 107:20 Ps 63:1-11
19 Matt 18:19 Eph 11:17 Ps 18:30	20 Mala 3:6 Gal 5:1 Ps 119:11	21 Ps 103 2Cor 10:4,5 Ps 119:50	22 Isa 53:5 Rmns 12:2 James 1:21	23 Jams 5:15,15 1John 5:4,5 Rmns 10:17	24 Prv 11:20,21 1John 5:12,13 Rmns 10:10	25 2Cor 12:10 3John 2 1Cor 13:13
26 Heb 11:6 Rmns 8:37 Ezek 12:25	27 Rmns 12:3 Prv 18:21 Dan 9:12	28 Rev 12:11 James 1:22 Matt 24:35	29 James 4:7 Josh 1:8 Rmns 4:21	30 Rmns 8:1,2 James 1:12 Rmns 10:9_	31 Rmns 12:1 Isa61:10 Acts 17:28	

August 2009 (Morning, Noon and Night)

Sunday	Monday	Tuesday	Wednesday	Thursday	Friday	Saturday
30 Ps 23 Matt 5:7 Eph 5:18	31 2Peter 3:14 Rmns 8:17 Heb 4:16					1 2Tim 1:12 Col 2:15 James 4:8
2 Rmns 8:2 Rmns 8:35 Heb 10:23	3 2Cor 5:17 Matt 18,19 Eph 5:30	4 James 1:12 Heb 4:12 Eph 1:7	5 Heb 1:3 1John 4:17 Mark 9:23	6 Rmns8:32 1John 3:8b Gal 2:20	7 1John 4:4 Col 2:15 Ps 91	8 Col 3:9,10 Rmns 8:37 Eph 3:17
9 Col 1:27 Josh 1:9 Rmns 8:31	10 Col 3:4 Jere 33:3 Heb 13:8	11 1Cor 1:30 John 15:7 Isa 54:17	12 2Cor 13:5 John 16:24 Philp 4:13	13 Heb 13:5,6 Philp 4:19 Eph 3:20	14 John 1:12 1Pet 2:24 Ps 118:24	15 Isa 41:10 Ps 107:20 Ps 63:1-11
16 Matt 18:19 Eph 11:17 Heb 4:15	17 Mala 3:6 Gal 5:1 Ps 62	18 Ps 103 2Cor 10:4,5 Rmns 6:14	19 Isa 53:5 Rmns 12:2 Luke 17:33	20 Jams 5:15,15 1John 5:4,5 John 3:29	21 Prv 11:20,21 1John 5:12,13 2Cor5:17	22 2Cor 12:10 3John 2 James 1:21
23 Heb 11:6 Rmns 8:37 Ezek 12:25	24 Rmns 12:3 Prv 18:21 Dan 9:12	25 Rev 12:11 James 1:22 Matt 24:35	26 James 4:7 Josh 1:8 Rmns 4:21	27 Rmns 8:1,2 James 1:12 Rmns 10:9_	28 Rmns 12:1 Isa61:10 Acts 17:28	29 Isa 44:3 Isa41:10 Isa59:1

September 2009 (Morning, Noon and Night)

Sunday	Monday	Tuesday	Wednesday	Thursday	Friday	Saturday
		1 Rmns 8:31 1John 3:8 1Peter 1:4	2 2Tim 1:12 Eph 1:3,4 Phil 4:19	3 Gal 2:20 1Cor 5:21 Col 1:13	4 Gal 3:13 1Cor 5:19 Col 2:15	5 Eze 36:26 Isa 49:25 Ps 46:10
6 Rmns 8:2 Rmns 8:35 Heb 10:23	7 2Cor 5:17 Matt 18,19 Eph 5:30	8 James 1:12 Heb 4:12 Eph 1:7	9 Heb 1:3 1John 4:17 Mark 9:23	10 Rmns8:32 1John 3:8b Gal 2:20	11 1John 4:4 Col 2:15 Ps 91	12 Col 3:9,10 Rmns 8:37 Eph 3:17
13 Col 1:27 Josh 1:9 Rmns 8:31	14 Col 3:4 Jere 33:3 Heb 13:8	15 1Cor 1:30 John 15:7 Isa 54:17	16 2Cor 13:5 John 16:24 Philp 4:13	17 Heb 13:5,6 Philp 4:19 Eph 3:20	18 John 1:12 1Pet 2:24 Ps 118:24	19 Isa 41:10 Ps 107:20 Ps 63:1-11
20 Matt 18:19 Eph 11:17 Ps 18:30	21 Mala 3:6 Gal 5:1 Ps 119:11	22 Ps 103 2Cor 10:4,5 Ps 119:50	23 Isa 53:5 Rmns 12:2 James 1:21	24 Jams 5:15,15 1John 5:4,5 Rmns 10:17	25 Prv 11:20,21 1John 5:12,13 Rmns 10:10	26 2Cor 12:10 3John 2 1Cor 13:13
27 Heb 11:6 Ezek 12:25 Rmns 10:9_	28 Rmns 12:3 Dan 9:12 Acts 17:28	29 Rev 12:11 Matt 24:35 Isa59:1	30 James 4:7 Rmns 4:21 Luke 6:35			

October 2009 (Morning, Noon and Night)

Sunday	Monday	Tuesday	Wednesday	Thursday	Friday	Saturday
				1 3John 2 2Tim 1:7 Mark 11:24	2 Mark 11:25,26 1John 3:8 Phil 4:19	3 2Tim 1:12 Eph 2:13 James 4:8
4 Rmns 8:2 Rmns 8:35 Heb 10:23	5 2Cor 5:17 Matt 18,19 Eph 5:30	6 James 1:12 Heb 4:12 Eph 1:7	7 Heb 1:3 1John 4:17 Mark 9:23	8 Rmns8:32 1John 3:8b Gal 2:20	9 1John 4:4 Col 2:15 Ps 91	10 Col 3:9,10 Rmns 8:37 Eph 3:17
11 Col 1:27 Josh 1:9 Rmns 8:31	12 Col 3:4 Jere 33:3 Heb 13:8	13 1Cor 1:30 John 15:7 Isa 54:17	14 2Cor 13:5 John 16:24 Philp 4:13	15 Heb 13:5,6 Philp 4:19 Eph 3:20	16 John 1:12 1Pet 2:24 Ps 118:24	17 Isa 41:10 Ps 107:20 Ps 63:1-11
18 Matt 18:19 Eph 11:17 Ps 18:30	19 Mala 3:6 Gal 5:1 Lam 3:22	20 Ps 103 2Cor 10:4,5 Matt 28:20	21 Isa 53:5 Rmns 12:2 Ps 103	22 Jams 5:15,15 1John 5:4,5 Rmns 10:17	23 Prv 11:20,21 1John 5:12,13 1Thess 5:23	24 2Cor 12:10 3John 2 John 10:10
25 Heb 11:6 Rmns 8:37 Ezek 12:25	26 Rmns 12:3 Prv 18:21 Dan 9:12	27 Rev 12:11 James 1:22 Matt 24:35	28 James 4:7 Josh 1:8 Rmns 4:21	29 Rmns 8:1,2 James 1:12 Rmns 10:9_	30 Rmns 12:1 Isa61:10 Acts 17:28	31 Isa 44:3 Isa41:10 Isa59:1

November 2009 (Morning, Noon and Night)

Sunday	Monday	Tuesday	Wednesday	Thursday	Friday	Saturday
1 Isa 55:1 Isa 44:2 Isa 43:7	2 Isa 43:1,-3 Isa 43:25 Isa 42:1	3 Isa 40:29 Isa 40:31 Isa 54:13	4 Isa 54:17 Isa 55:6 Isa 55:3	5 Isa 55:8,9 Isa 55:11 1Peter 1:4	6 John 6:63 1John 3:8 Phil 4:19	7 Rmns 8:31 Col 2:15 James 4:8
8 Rmns 8:2 Rmns 8:35 Heb 10:23	9 2Cor 5:17 Matt 18,19 Eph 5:30	10 James 1:12 Heb 4:12 Eph 1:7	11 Heb 1:3 1John 4:17 Mark 9:23	12 Rmns8:32 1John 3:8b Gal 2:20	13 1John 4:4 Col 2:15 Ps 91	14 Col 3:9,10 Rmns 8:37 Eph 3:17
15 Col 1:27 Josh 1:9 Rmns 8:31	16 Col 3:4 Jere 33:3 Heb 13:8	17 1Cor 1:30 John 15:7 Isa 54:17	18 2Cor 13:5 John 16:24 Philp 4:13	19 Heb 13:5,6 Philp 4:19 Eph 3:20	20 John 1:12 1Pet 2:24 Ps 118:24	21 Isa 41:10 Ps 107:20 Ps 63:1-11
22 Matt 18:19 Eph 11:17 Ps 18:30	23 Mala 3:6 Gal 5:1 Rmns 10:10	24 Ps 103 2Cor 10:4,5 1Cor 13:13	25 Isa 53:5 Rmns 12:2 1Cor 8:6	26 Jams 5:15,15 1John 5:4,5 1Peter 2:9	27 Prv 11:20,21 1John 5:12,13 Eph 1:5	28 2Cor 12:10 3John 2 Php 2:5
29 Heb 11:6 Rmns 8:37 Ezek 12:25	30 Rmns 12:3 Prv 18:21 Dan 9:12					

December 2009 (Morning, Noon and Night)

Sunday	Monday	Tuesday	Wednesday	Thursday	Friday	Saturday
		1 Isa 56:15 Isa 59:21 Isa 59:1	2 Rmns 8:31 2Tim 1:12 1John 4:17	3 1John 3:8 Col 2:15 1Peter 1:4	4 Phil 4:19 James 4:8 Phil 4:19	5 1John 5:5 1John 5:20 Acts 2:38
6 Rmns 8:2 Rmns 8:35 Heb 10:23	7 2Cor 5:17 Matt 18,19 Eph 5:30	8 James 1:12 Heb 4:12 Eph 1:7	9 Heb 1:3 1John 4:17 Mark 9:23	10 Rmns8:32 1John 3:8b Gal 2:20	11 1John 4:4 Col 2:15 Ps 91	12 Col 3:9,10 Rmns 8:37 Eph 3:17
13 Col 1:27 Josh 1:9 Rmns 8:31	14 Col 3:4 Jere 33:3 Heb 13:8	15 1Cor 1:30 John 15:7 Isa 54:17	16 2Cor 13:5 John 16:24 Philp 4:13	17 Heb 13:5,6 Philp 4:19 Eph 3:20	18 John 1:12 1Pet 2:24 Ps 118:24	19 Isa 41:10 Ps 107:20 Ps 63:1-11
20 Matt 18:19 Eph 11:17 Ps 18:30	21 Mala 3:6 Gal 5:1 Ps 119:11	22 Ps 103 2Cor 10:4,5 James 1:21	23 Isa 53:5 Rmns 12:2 Matt 1:23	24 Matt 4:4 Matt 7:7,8 Matt 7:12	25 Prv 11:20,21 1John 5:12,13 Matt 8:17	26 2Cor 12:10 3John 2 Matt11:28
27 Heb 11:6 Rmns 8:37 Ezek 12:25	28 Rmns 12:3 Prv 18:21 Dan 9:12	29 Rev 12:11 James 1:22 Matt 24:35	30 James 4:7 Josh 1:8 Rmns 4:21	31 Matt 21:21 James 1:12 John 10:10_		

138

Chapter 29

Spiritual Warfare

Put on the whole Armour of God. Ephesians 6:11-17

"No weapon that is formed against you shall prosper."
Isaiah 54:17a

Chapter 30

GRACE

"Grace is what you have to write this book."

"Grace is what brought you here and "Grace will bring you home," says "The Lord God. "

And Jesus said, "I see Grace flowing from the throne room of God;" These are showers of blessings of Grace from God, to supply my need for that day; and would receive Grace on a daily basis. They are new every morning.

I was wondering just what does Grace include? And what does it mean by the word "Grace,"
What do you think it means?

The Vines dictionary says "it's Divine favor"; which I have heard and assumed all my life; and that's all. There has to be more, I thought.

It was on August 4, 2020, "Jesus explained the word Grace, which includes several things; "Like strength and endurance for All your tasks; and Peace goes along with it. Peace always goes together with Grace because God has Himself wrapped up in that greeting."

Jesus also defined Grace for me "as a Companion, even the Closest Companion;" for He said, "I will go with you wherever you go."

I was sharing with someone that I'm writing a Book, and the person asked ,"What is it all about?

"I said that God was teaching me about the Love of God and of His Son." The Person responded ,"Oh AGAPE"; referring to a kind of love.

Now, I've heard this all my life and it came up again in my mind later in the day. So I asked Jesus, "Did you ever use the word AGAPE?" He said, " No,never. I used Grace." And you can quote that too, in your book."

I was still curious and looked up the word AGAPE in the Vine's Dictionary, and it says:

"AGAPE is used in the plural in Jude 12, and some in 2Peter 2:13; In the margin, "many ancient authorities read, "Decevings,"; (apatais) so as "These love- feats arose from the common meals of the early church. (1Corinthians 11:21).

They may have had their origin in the private meals of the Jewish household, with the addition of the observance of the Lord's Supper.

However, there were similar common meals among the pagan brotherhoods. The evil dealt with Corinth became enhanced by the presence of immoral persons, who degraded the feats into wanton banquets, as mentioned in 2Peter and Jude. In later times the agape became detached from the Lord's Supper."

Jesus is exactly like it says He is. Loving, caring, compassionate, long suffering, Prince of Peace, Counselor, Knows All;

Like He has said to me, " nothing passes Him by." Almighty God, Everlasting Father; And has plenty of Grace for everyone in the whole world, whom He has Loved and created.

If you don't have a friend like I have, His name is Jesus; and He will be there to greet you with open arms, when you call upon him."He said He will no way cast you out.

You have never known the kind of love that He has for you; it's so warm and loving, beyond my description; and what He says, He will do. It's all true. This friend of mine you can trust.

I will lift up my eyes unto the hills, from whence cometh my help. My help comes from the Lord, which made heaven and earth." Psalm 121:1,2

So, after all is said and done, what is God telling us about His Love?

Jesus was present and said, "The Love of God is the essence of life." What does essence mean, I asked? "Life is dependent on God's Love." AMEN AND AMEN.

Chapter 31

In Remembrance of my sister, Janet

From 1965 to 1978, a possible fourteen years, my older sister Janet, had served our family Thanksgiving Meals. It included our parents, and their 6 children; Janet being the oldest. Me, Donna, and my husband had 4 children; 2 boys and 2 girls.

When Janet got married, and had their first child, moved to another state, and their family grew to be five children. A girl and 4 boys. So it was our family that was invited the night before Thanksgiving at Janet's house.

Their house was a two story with a sunporch and a basement. So when we got together with their 5 and our 4 children, it didn't seem crowded. The boys were on couches and the basement. We had the second floor with the girls, and us and Janet with our spouses.

The rest of the family arrived on Thanksgiving day. Which included our parents, and three brothers that were married and the youngest, single daughter, who got married later.

Oh, our son's Birthday is celebrated every year there and he recalls A donut with a candle instead of a cake.

Janet and her husband always provided two turkeys, and her husband's job was to base them; and the aroma was strong when we awoke; but Janet's gravy was perfect and always made plenty.

We would have games like:

Foosball; and I recall Lora brought a paper game of Christmas quotes to fill in the answers for the adults; the men watched football.

Mom and Dad looked at pictures; and the two cousin daughters provided skits and songs with piano. Dad was a quiet person but liked football with the others too.

It was a Tradition to have a Swedish drink, called Glug, which was a nice hot drink on a cold day that my brother really looked forward to; I also made lapel pins for a while for the women to wear.

The table was set with the best dishes and goblets; the children were small when we started, so there was a couple of makeshift tables for them.

After the meal the women did the clean up and dishes, then the children got all bundled up to go on the other tradition, even when it was cold, they would take the long walk downhill to the river. When they got down there and were ready to hike back, soon we would get a call on the phone, saying, "Come and get us.!!

The two, girl, cousins would entertain us with skits and singing, familiar Musical Hits.

One time they made up Commercials which was quite cute. Years later one of the High School students sang his lead song in "Music Man," "There's trouble in River City."

Speaking of musicals, both Janet and I were in Operettas. Janet was in "Prince of Pillson," and I was in two Operettas; "The Chocolate Soldier" and "Sweethearts."

As years went by, the family grew to be 32 people, so we decided to stop having Thanksgiving at Janet's house. But the memories are still fresh in our hearts.

It wasn't very long until Janet's husband Glen died. So with Glen gone, as well as the children being older and having left the nest, she was happy to look for a new house.

We always wrote letters to each other at least once a week, to keep in touch.

My husband's parents were in the South, so we would stop in to see Janet on the way.

It's always a warm happy greeting to see each other, and again, she had a room for us to stay the night. We watch TV or a game and always have a piece of pie before bed time. Our return trip back home was the same.

This was a habit for several years, stopping on our way down south and back, to see my sister Janet.

Several years went by and Janet got Parkinson's disease, and needed to go into a Nursing home. So on our way south we'd stopped in to see her there.

She had a nice room. I noticed her favorite large living room picture over her bed. Her rocking chair nearby, a TV and a big closet.

Oh, warm hugs and smiles were our first happy greetings, and her eyes just sparkled.

The next year we stopped in to see Janet, as we traveled south; but this visit will be different.

We went in the door we did the last time there, but she wasn't in the same room as before.

She had been moved to another station; so we weren't sure what was up.

The first thing she said, as I stooped down to get close to hear her speak, as she said, with a raspy quiet voice "This is what happens when your money runs out."

Well I don't know about that, but I do know she probably needed to be watched; as she falls out of bed. Like she said, "I'm wired."

I glanced over the divided room, with a curtain between, as she had a roommate.

Her bed was close to the door; a lamp on the small table next to her, was a small family picture; below her bed was half a closet, with 3 drawers below. Next to that was the sink and one toilet room. A Shower was elsewhere and the TV was in the gathering area.

Our visit wasn't too long and as we said our Goodbyes, I turned to leave and I heard her say, "Write to me every day, would you?" What? Okay! I said." So I did .

Her Son told me later, that she's living her life through me; meaning through my letters. That's an awesome thing. That change must have been dramatic for her to say that.

However, pretty soon she wrote and said "Stop! I don't have the room for all these letters." So I wrote less often; and Janet's oldest son, said "she's doing better and getting used to the routine."

He brings his phone with him when he goes to see her; and he would hold the phone up to her ear so we could hear each other. I thought that was so special of him to do that for us. Time flew and as years quickly go by; because I believe she was in the Nursing Home for seven years.

So one day her Son called me and said I think she's dying; and Later that day, I found out that she had.

I'm telling you all of this because in the end, there is a Moral to tell, if you stick with me on this.

Janet's daughter made all the arrangements for the funeral. Our daughter drove me and my husband to attend.

All of Janet's boys, four of them were there, and since my husband and I were out of towners, we didn't know anyone except the family.

It was very nice, and at the end of the service there was a surprise; Janet was on tape and sang the "Lord's prayer."

Both my daughter and I looked at each other at the same time, because we were in awe that she started the music high; and we both were waiting to see if she could finish high, which she did with no effort. We all had forgotten she was a Lyric Soprano, and It was lovely.

Chapter 32

The Miracle Yellow Rose

A s Everyone filed out, we passed the casket and were told beforehand, that we each can take a rose, which we did. They were all yellow and very big; I think it was 4" wide with a long stem.

Now our trip home was six hours; so I was looking for something to put both roses in; and I saw a water bottle that had water already in it. Both roses were in the bottle for the six hour drive. When we arrived home, my daughter said I could keep them both. Now I know roses last about a week or so; therefore I didn't plan on changing the water.

They were a beautiful 4" wide yellow roses, so I took a picture right away and placed them beneath the bow window in the living room; and the light seemed sufficient there.

About a little over a week I noticed that one of the roses dropped down, just like I thought it would. It was no doubt, dead.

I looked at the other rose as I passed by as another week had gone by, and it's looking pretty good yet. So I think I'll keep an eye on you.

And another week went on and I decided I better keep track of just how many days it's been; and keep watching.

15th Day

Now it's The 15th day and I guess I must have missed something, because when I looked closer I saw new leaves! 5 New Leaves? On a long stemmed Rose?

20th Day

Five days go by and I see something new. All the petals look crinkly, all shriveled looking. Maybe crinkly is the word? But It's still straight up and not drooping at all.

I want to remind you that I never added any water as I didn't want to touch it; and just how long this is going to take to die, I have no idea.; because I just didn't expect it to last this long.

So I said to the Lord, "What are you trying to tell me? He answered, "You'll see." So I waited some more.

30th Day

Another ten days went by and I looked at the rose and said, "I know you should be dead by now, even though you don't look like it; So I'm going to bury the Rose now; and look at you! you're still standing straight up, but crinkly."

Chapter 33

The Moral

A fter I buried the rose I said to the Lord, "Okay, what are you telling me." Then the Lord answered and said

"It's just because, as you showed your faithfulness to your sister, I wanted to show you how faithful I am to you; As it is written: "As you did it to the least of these, you did it unto Me." Matthew 25:40

CPSIA information can be obtained
at www.ICGtesting.com
Printed in the USA
BVHW041729190122
626641BV00007B/55